HMS Endurance
The Red Plum

"By Endurance we Conquer"

Graham Smith

For the officers and ratings of HMS Endurance, Past, Present and Future

HMS Endurance
The Red Plum

Graham Smith

COACH HOUSE PUBLICATIONS
Isle of Wight
England

Copyright © Coach House Publications Limited 2006

Photographs © Crown Copyright 2006

Except where indicated

All rights reserved. No part of this work covered by the copyrights hereon may be reproduced or used in any form or by any means - graphic, electronic or mechanical, including photocopying, recording, taping of information on storage and retrieval systems - without the prior written permission of the publisher.

Front Cover Photograph, HMS Endurance alongside King Edward Point, South Georgia

ISBN: 1-899-392-467

COACH HOUSE PUBLICATIONS LIMITED

ISLE OF WIGHT, ENGLAND

The Coach House, School Green Road, Freshwater, Isle of Wight, PO40 9BB
Tel: +44 (0) 1983 755655

Further copies of this book can be obtained from the publishers by contacting us at the address above
or via our online ordering service at www.coachhouseonline.co.uk

Printed in the UK
Book Design by David Bowles

Table of Contents

7	Foreword by Captain Nick Lambert **HMS Endurance**	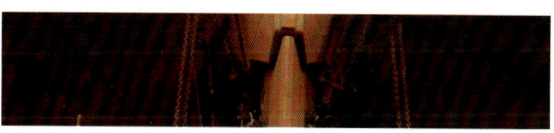
8–15	CHAPTER ONE **The Ship**	
16–21	CHAPTER TWO **Endurances Past**	
22–39	CHAPTER THREE **The Plum**	
40–77	CHAPTER FOUR **Endurance at Work**	
78–93	CHAPTER FIVE **Where she goes**	
95	Further information and Acknowledgements	

Foreword

The United Kingdom has been involved in Antarctic exploration and science for over 200 years, with the Royal Navy playing a formative role from the earliest forays into the southern ocean and especially during the first decades of the 20th Century. From James Cook and James Clark Ross, to Captain Scott, Shackleton (whose family motto *'by endurance we conquer'* determined our name) and, more recently, Captain Nick Barker, the Royal Navy has been intimately involved in matters Antarctica. Ships of the Royal Navy pepper the history of the continent – among many others *HMS Resolution*, *HMS Terror* and *HMS Erebus* in the earliest days to *HMS Protector* and *HMS Endurance* in the latter half of the last century – emphasising the contribution of our illustrious predecessors and providing the inspiration for geographical features such as Mount Erebus on the shores of the Ross Sea.

Aboard the present *Endurance* we often worry that we use the term 'unique' too frequently but it is a fact that our ship and her role are indeed unique, arguably on a national basis and certainly within the Royal Navy. She is, we believe, a national asset funded originally by the Treasury and tasked by four main stakeholders – the Foreign and Commonwealth Office (FCO), the British Antarctic Survey (BAS), the UK Hydrographic Office (UKHO) and, of course, the Ministry of Defence. Her mission *'to patrol and survey the Antarctic and South Atlantic maintaining sovereign presence with defence diplomacy and supporting the global community of Antarctica'* encapsulates the requirements of those stakeholders and describes the planning that underpins her annual deployments to the harsh environment of Antarctica.

We deploy, of course, in much greater comfort than our predecessors and, aided by modern technology, can plot the seabed in three dimensional colour or determine position within centimetres but the purposes of exploration and science remain as inextricably intertwined as they have through history. The exploration is somewhat different, focused on accurate charting of little known and often treacherous waters; whilst the science builds on the work of our forebears, progressing knowledge of our planet and environment with a contemporary emphasis on global warming and climate change. Our intimate relationship with our stakeholders ensures that our resources are used to best effect - be it inspecting oft visited tourist sites or scientific bases for the FCO under the auspices of the Antarctic Treaty, supporting BAS fieldcamps in remote locations or surveying safe routes for cruise ships at the behest of the UKHO – and reflects the Royal Navy's global role as a versatile maritime force acting for good in the world.

I'm privileged to be drafting the foreword to this excellent book which captures the history, capability and output of the third *Endurance*. We cannot claim the persistence, bravery or privations of our predecessors but we have the honour to follow in their footsteps, to glimpse the conditions in which they strove and to build on their work in Antarctica.

Captain Nick Lambert
HMS Endurance
August, 2006

CHAPTER ONE

The Ship

Whether anyone has sailed in one or not, there is an image of a Royal Navy ship that most people have in their mind. Sleek, grey and fast. Sharp-profiled and bristling with sophisticated weapons, systems and sensors. Ready to take on all comers.

But this one is different. HMS *Endurance* is a ship like no other. She may be a unit of Her Majesty's Royal Navy, but she has a bright red and white paint scheme rather than the warlike grey of her cousins. She does have an unusual array of sensors – but they are used to examine the world above and below her rather than to seek out enemy vessels. And she carries no weapons apart from a few small arms. Even her ice-modified Lynx helicopters fly unarmed.

She's a British naval vessel that was built as civilian ice-breaker in a Norwegian shipyard. She's a naval vessel that doesn't operate in a task force but works independently, in some of the wildest and most remote places in the world. The people and organisations she supports aren't other warships but are research organisations, scientists, weather forecasters, cartographers and remote communities. She's one of a kind. But make no mistake – she is Navy through and through. Her ship's complement comes to her from all parts of the service, including the Royal Marines, and most have served on bases and warships in Britain and around the world.

HMS *Endurance* is the Royal Navy's sole Ice Patrol Ship and, although based in Portsmouth, spends more than half of each year operating in the stormy seas and lonely places of the Antarctic. Her mission is: 'To patrol and survey the Antarctic and South Atlantic, maintaining Sovereign Presence with Defence Diplomacy and supporting the global community of Antarctica'.

CHAPTER ONE - **The Ship**

She was built in Norway by Ulstein Hatlo and launched in 1990 as M.V. *Polar Circle*. Originally intended for Antarctic shipping specialists Rieber Lines she was chartered by the Royal Navy in 1991 and entered service then as HMS *Polar Circle*. Shortly afterwards the Ministry of Defence purchased her outright and renamed her HMS *Endurance* – the second Royal Navy ship to bear the name. The Navy also gave her the motto *Fortitudine Vincimus* (By Endurance We Conquer), which was Sir Ernest Shackleton's family motto and used by him on his 1914-5 Imperial Trans-Antarctic Expedition.

So what does she do?

Flexible, capable and unique, HMS *Endurance* covers some 32,000 km (20,000 miles) every year on a 6-7 month deployment, patrolling remote waters, promoting the UK's interests and supporting many kinds of scientific research.

Her direct responsibilities to government include a remit from the Foreign and Commonwealth Office (FCO) to promote British interests in the Antarctic and South Atlantic, to regularly survey British facilities and to patrol isolated coastlines and islands. In her Defence Diplomacy role her ship's company become ambassadors for the UK by visiting foreign ports, where they create relationships and build links with governments, navies and people.

Another significant customer, or stakeholder, is the UK Hydrographic Office (UKHO), a government Trading Fund and part of the Ministry of Defence. The UKHO's primary role is the provision of navigation information for mariners, in the form of charts, guides, databases and other media. The UKHO's major customers are the Royal Navy and merchant marine, but their products are used all around the world by commercial, naval and tourist maritime operators. *Endurance* is tasked by the UKHO with collecting data on the structure of the seabed, and taking depth soundings in coastal regions, inlets, bays and natural harbours. This data is used to update and improve charts and navigation information – a service that is becoming ever more important with the exponential increase in Antarctic tourism.

The Meteorological (Met) Office is another Ministry of Defence Trading Fund, this time with the role of providing weather information and forecasting to help mariners, aviators and others carry out their business safely and effectively. While at sea *Endurance's* Hydrography and Meteorology team takes regular measurements of sea temperature, salinity, currents, wind and general weather conditions. Over time their observations improve our understanding of weather systems and help make the world's oceans safer for travel and commerce.

CHAPTER ONE - The Ship

Improved understanding of the natural world is a common theme of many of Endurance's activities. And it is also the remit of another stakeholder, the British Antarctic Survey (BAS). BAS is part of the UK's Natural Environment Research Council and maintains a series of research programmes within British Antarctic Territory. BAS runs a number of permanent and summer-only stations and field surveys, and *Endurance* and her helicopters play an important role in supporting these. Much of this scientific effort is concerned with understanding the Antarctic environment, leading to greater understanding of the global ecosystem and the impact human activity has on it.

While these are the main stakeholders, *Endurance* usually has many other tasks to fulfil while on deployment. A recent example includes helping a BBC film crew to take spectacular aerial views for a major wildlife documentary. Other media support roles have included taking journalists to BAS stations and transporting a wildlife photographer working on a book on the natural life in South Georgia

But that's not all. *Endurance* has also:

- Supported an Antarctic exploration and adventure expedition made up of young people selected from thousands of applicants from schools around the UK.
- Delivered building materials to repair and preserve a historic building at an abandoned whaling station, now a tourist site
- Hosted an FCO-led multi-national inspection team whose job is to create guidelines under the auspices of the Antarctic Treaty for sites regularly visited by tourist ships.

International cooperation runs like a thread through all operations in the Antarctic. With the creation of the Antarctic Charter, over 20 countries have agreed to set aside national claims to work together to preserve the region and prevent the destruction of its environment by excessive commercial pressures. Countries run joint scientific studies, and national research organisations share transport and resources where needed. And at the most basic level, those working in this hostile environment will always assist each other when problems and emergencies occur.

HMS *Endurance* plays a vital role in all of this – as ambassador, explorer, surveyor and transport. And doing all this while operating in some of the most hostile and dangerous places in the world, full of hazards for the unprepared. Challenging and complex, yes, but a challenge that *Endurance* and her professional and dedicated crew step up to every time they set sail.

HMS *Endurance* at work on the ice with one of the BAS supply ships

CHAPTER TWO

Endurances Past

Today's *Endurance* isn't the first ship to bear that name, nor is she the first to serve in the Royal Navy.

The first *Endurance* was a civilian ship and took part in an epic journey of exploration, survival and heroism. As with today's vessel she was built in a Norwegian shipyard, although she was a lot smaller, with a displacement of only 350 tons. Wooden-hulled, her propulsion was a coal-fired triple-expansion steam engine and her barquentine sailing rig. She was originally known as *Polaris* and was purchased by Ernest Shackleton for his 1914 British Imperial Trans-Antarctic Expedition. Shackleton renamed her *Endurance* from his family motto *Fortitudine Vincimus* (By Endurance We Conquer).

Born in Ireland in 1874 and brought up in England, Ernest Shackleton was one of those restless adventurers that made their mark on the Victorian era. He first went to sea at the age of 16 and gained his master's ticket by 24. But the life of a merchant seafarer wasn't enough for him and in 1901 Shackleton signed up for Robert Scott's expedition to the South Pole. They failed to reach the Pole, although Shackleton, Scott and Dr Edward Wilson did get to within 772 km (480 miles), much further south than anyone else had reached at the time. Shackleton was subsequently invalided home, suffering from scurvy-like symptoms.

Shackleton had by now developed a taste for such exploration so organised his own 1907 British Antarctic Expedition, usually known (from the name of his ship) as the *Nimrod* expedition. During this attempt Shackleton travelled further south than anyone else had achieved, and got to within 180 km (112 miles) of the Pole before being forced to turn back.

In 1914 Shackleton was able to get the financial backing to lead yet another expedition. But in the

Ernest Shackleton whose family motto is, Fortitudine Vincimus
By Endurance We Conquer seen here (on the right)
with Geologist James Wordie

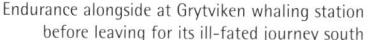

Endurance alongside at Grytviken whaling station
before leaving for its ill-fated journey south

Photographs © PJ Wordie

Chapter Two - Endurance's Past

intervening years the South Pole had finally been reached by the Norwegian Roald Amundsen, in a race with Scott, who had died, along with his men, on the return journey. Shackleton decided to go a step further and this time cross the Antarctic continent from sea to sea via the South Pole. One group of men were to sail to the Ross Sea to position stores on the that side of the route, while the larger group, under Shackleton, were to take *Endurance* into the Weddell Sea as far as they could before completing the journey by dog-towed sledge.

With a crew of 28 men (including one stowaway) and under the command of her Master, Frank Worsley, the *Endurance* set off in August 1914 just as war was breaking out. After stopping for resupply and the latest ice information at the whaling stations in South Georgia, they set off for the Weddell Sea on December 5. It quickly became apparent that the ice conditions were much worse than expected and the ship was only ably to grind forward slowly. The ice thickened, until by December 19, she became completely stuck. Although Shackleton's *Endurance* was extremely strongly built, her deep 'V' hull profile meant that she was gripped solidly by the ice rather than being able to rise and settle on the ice surface in the manner of today's 'U'-shaped icebreakers.

The crew adapted, living from the ship as if she were an ice-bound base camp, trying to preserve their stores of food for as long as they could. Ship and ice drifted together, with occasional attempts by the crew to break free and sail on. They remained like this until October 1915, when increasing ice pressure caused the hull to crack and spring leaks. The crushing force increased, until, on 21 November, after her crew had removed all useful stores and equipment, *Endurance* finally sank.

They then began an epic trek, manhandling their essential supplies and the ship's three lifeboats across the ice, trying to reach the open sea. It took them until April 9, 1916 before they were able to safely launch the ship's boats, by when they had spent 156 days on the ice.

A seven-day sea crossing ensued, with the small open boats dodging icebergs and fighting storms, and the men enduring hunger, thirst, illness and seasickness. They eventually made landfall on the rocky coast of Elephant Island, where a base camp and hut was created using the upturned hulls of two of the lifeboats, lifted on to low walls built from stones. But the hardest part of the journey was yet to come.

Wood salvaged from two of the boats was used to make repairs and create a covered space and mast on the third boat, the *James Caird*. Shackleton and five other men intended to sail this tiny 7 m (23 ft) open boat to the Stromness Whaling Station at South Georgia, through 1,280 km (800 miles) of freezing, wild storm-tossed sea.

Endurance's name laid out in stone on the hillside overlooking
Port Stanley in the Falkland Islands

In the cemetary above the old whaling station in Grytviken,
South Georgia lies Shackleton's Grave, facing South
towards the Pole

Photographs © Tony Hall

Chapter Two - Endurance's Past

They launched on Easter Monday, April 24, 1916. For the next 17 days, the *James Caird* made an average of 95–115 km (60–70 miles) per day, pitching and rolling, with waves constantly breaking over her. By a combination of luck, courage and sheer bloody-minded refusal to give in, the crew eventually reached land at King Haakon Bay on the west side of South Georgia – a remarkable feat of seamanship and navigation. There the exhausted men sheltered under the upturned hull of their boat and tried to regain some strength by catching and eating albatrosses and their eggs.

But they still had to reach the whaling station on the far side of the island. Their boat was no longer seaworthy so their only recourse was to cross South Georgia's interior and 41 km (26 miles) of unmapped mountains, rocks, glaciers and crevasses. On May 9, 1916, three men, Shackleton, Frank Worsley and Tom Crean, set off. The men were already weak and suffering from malnutrition, exhaustion and frostbite, while their only mountaineering equipment was 15m (50 ft) of rope, a carpenter's adze for an ice axe, and screws through the soles of their boots as makeshift crampons. After 36 hours of struggling through some of the wildest and unforgiving terrain in the world, the three filthy, ragged, wild-haired men staggered into the whaling station they had left so optimistically 17 months earlier.

Shackleton was quickly able to arrange a boat from the whaling station to sail around the island to pick up the three men left behind at King Haakon Bay. It took longer to organise a rescue for the main group on Elephant Island, but by August 30, 1916, Shackleton eventually got to them in the *Yelcho*, a tug volunteered by the Chilean government. Some of the survivors were ill, some had frostbite, some had lost toes, and all were heartily sick of seal blubber and penguin meat – but everyone who set out on the *Endurance* had survived. When the whole group got back to Puntas Arenas, they were feted as heroes. Back home in Britain, newspapers will filled with stories of their heroic exploits as a happy counter to the grim news from the war.

However, Shackleton still had another rescue to mount. The group that had sailed to the Ross Sea were also stranded and in trouble. Their ship, *Aurora*, had been torn free in bad weather and the crew on board were barely able to sail her to safety, leaving 10 men ashore in conditions similar to those on Elephant Island. Shackleton eventually returned with the refitted Aurora to rescue them, although three had died in the meantime – the only casualties of his failed expedition.

In later years Shackleton continued to explore, and eventually died on January 5, 1922, during another expedition to the south. He is buried at South Georgia, and his grave site is usually visited by the crew of today's *Endurance* when she calls in at the island.

CHAPTER TWO - Endurance's Past

Endurance goes to war

The first *HMS Endurance* to serve in the Royal Navy was originally the Anita Dan, a 3,500-tonne Danish-built icebreaker owned by the Lauritzen Line. She was purchased by the United Kingdom in 1967 and modified to become the Royal Navy's Ice Patrol Ship.

In 1982 Argentina launched a military invasion of South Georgia and the Falkland Islands, when the lightly armed *Endurance* was the only Royal Navy presence in the region. She stayed in the area to provide reconnaissance, and used her Wasp helicopters to land Marines to retake South Georgia. Her helicopters also took part in the successful attacks on the Argentinean submarine, the Santa Fe. As an integrated element of the Royal Navy task force, *Endurance* later landed Marines and Special Forces on the Falklands themselves. For her services the ship was later awarded the Wilkinson Sword of Peace, and this, together with her 1982 battle honour, sits in a glass case in today's *Endurance*. The table in the wardroom of today's vessel is also from her predecessor and was the table on which the Argentine's surrender of South Georgia was signed in April 1982.

Endurance was eventually withdrawn from service in 1991 and her replacement is the subject of this book.

Previous *HMS Endurance* Photo by Alan Broomhead

THE RED PLUM   21   HMS Endurance

Chapter Three

The Plum

HMS *Endurance* was originally built in Norway by Ulstein Hatlo as a class 1 icebreaker; a background that defines her shape, her structure and her build. Her appearance is civilian, with a rounded, high-profile hull topped by a high, squared superstructure. Large squared-off windows give superb visibility from the bridge and upper superstructure, while plenty smaller ones provide light to much of the accommodation and workspaces. Her colour scheme of a bright red hull and gleaming white superstructure certainly makes her stand out, whether against ice or sea. Her predecessor wore the same scheme, and both ships ended up with the perhaps inevitable nickname of 'The Red Plum'.

Such a broad hull and flat underside prevents her being gripped tightly by ice and crushed, unlike Shackleton's *Endurance*. It also allows her to break through ice by driving up on to it and crushing down to create a free channel. Her ice-breaking capability demands a smooth hull with no protrusions, apart from a steel blade under the bow which initiates the crack in the ice. The smooth hull also means there are no stabilisers to help with rough seas, although to dampen her motion when the sea gets up she does have a stabilising tank holding up to 60 tonnes of water. But she still has a reputation for rolling in heavy weather and can be uncomfortable for those with less robust 'sea legs'.

That aside, *Endurance* is comfortable to sail and work in. Her accommodation is comparatively spacious to compared that in a warship and her wide passageways are more akin to those on a civilian ferry. Pipes and cabling are hidden behind boxed conduits while many of the living spaces and cabins have carpeted floors. The few watertight hatches are mainly to the outside of the superstructure and the ship doesn't have quite the same physical compartmentalisation that a vessel designed for combat has. Even so, she does have six large

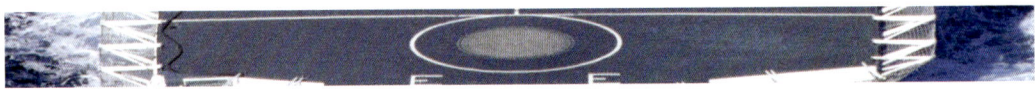

Displacement:
6,000 tons
Length:
91 m (299 ft)
Beam:
17.9 m (58.7 ft)
Draught:
8.5 m (27.9 ft)
Top speed:
14 knots
Cruise speed:
12 knots
Crew:
118
(including 6 Royal Marines)
Aircraft:
2 x Lynx Mk III helicopters
Boats:
2 x Survey Motor Boats
5 x boats

CHAPTER THREE - **The Plum**

sliding doors that can be activated in an emergency from the bridge. Powerful hydraulics push them closed to divide the ship into sealed areas and restrict the area affected by any flooding or fire.

Unlike most 'grey' warships, HMS *Endurance* has plenty of deck space. Leading back from the foremast and raised foc'sle deck at the bow, a large open foredeck holds the McGregor access hatch for the main hold. On the starboard side is the support cradle for *Nimrod*, one of her Survey Motor Boats (SMB). Two smaller boats known as RIBs (Rigid Inflatable Boats) sit in movable cradles on the port side, one usually placed on top of the McGregor hatch. A large crane is mounted on the foredeck, used for loading and unloading the hold and for launching and retrieving the boats. Extra storage containers can also be mounted on top of the McGregor hatch.

Immediately behind the foredeck is the vertical face of the superstructure, towering up over five stories to the bridge. The rear half of the superstructure is largely taken up by the aircraft hangar, which is slightly offset to starboard. On the port side of this is the exhaust stack for the main engines and other systems, which leads up to a squat squared-off funnel. Two more boats and their davits are alongside this stack, just to the rear of the main superstructure. The forward boat is SMB *James Caird*, and behind it is the Captain's launch, the *Eddie Shackleton*. Further towards the stern, adjacent to the main hangar door, is the flight deck, complete with railings that fold down when flying takes place. The flight deck is also used for diplomatic receptions and sporting events.

Below this flight deck is another open space, the quarterdeck. Partially roofed by the flight deck, it is open to starboard and the stern, but enclosed to port and forward by the superstructure. The quarterdeck is usually where visitors arrive when Endurance is in port, but it has a multitude of other uses. As the only large, but sheltered, open space, the quarterdeck is a venue for training exercises, religious and military ceremonies and leisure events such as barbecues.

Engine room

The heart of the ship is the main engine room, built around two Bergen marine diesels. A Norwegian company currently owned by Rolls-Royce, Bergen has a long history of developing and manufacturing marine power plants. Two Bergen BRGs are on board *Endurance*, giving her a shaft output of 8,160 horsepower – about 100 times the power of a typical family car. Each engine has eight cylinders in a single line, and they are bigger than almost any other Royal Navy diesel, except for those in the amphibious assault ships HMS *Ocean* and *Albion*, and the Hydrographic Survey ship HMS *Scott*. Both engines drive into one gearbox, which in turn drives the single propeller shaft. Such a configuration enables the

Chapter Three - The Plum

ship to run on one engine for economy but allows the crew to easily 'clutch-in' the second engine when more power is needed.

The main Engine Room follows civilian style containing virtually all the propulsion-related machinery (unlike on fighting warships, where vital equipment is distributed around the ship). It is a noisy place with at least one engine operating at all times while at sea. Perhaps surprisingly, the room temperature can vary widely, from the high 40s in the tropics to nearly freezing when in Antarctica.

Immediately next to the main Engine Room is the Engine Control Room (ECR). Someone is always on watch here, using the various computer systems to monitor the engines and much of the ship's electrical and mechanical machinery.

While the main engines can operate within a reasonable range of revolutions per minute (RPM) they are at their most efficient and economical within a narrow RPM band. So, as with most ships, the engine room crew try to keep the engines working at a constant speed as far as possible. To allow a range of sailing speeds, the main screw is fitted with four blades that can be set to different angles to produce more or less thrust. These Variable Pitch (VP) blades are hydraulically operated, from an actuator that runs down the centre of the main drive shaft. Variable pitch means that when the bridge asks for a particular speed, it's the blade angle that is changed more than the engine speed.

Blocks of hardened ice can be a hazard to whirling blades so the screw has a large, cylindrical metal cowl around it to protect it. And in confined spaces, the main screw and rudder are supplemented by bow and stern thrusters for precise positioning, such as when berthing alongside. Shielded behind grilles flush beneath the hull, they are powered from the main engines, but are only effective at speeds of less than four knots.

Range

Endurance carries up to 1,200 cubic metres of diesel fuel oil – that's 1,200,000 litres or about 1020 tonnes. With her engines operating at their most economical settings, one load of fuel can theoretically take her some 44,000 km (24,000 nautical miles): enough to take her easily around the world. That's the theory anyway. In practice, different modes of operation can increase fuel usage. Ice-breaking creates especially high levels of consumption as the engines use maximum power to move the ship slowly and not very far. And no Captain will want to run the tanks down to empty – partly because it leaves no operational flexibility and partly because the weight of the fuel itself contributes to the stability of the ship in rough seas. On deployment *Endurance* will refuel several times, usually in the Falkland Islands.

Chapter Three - The Plum

Power for living and working

Motive power is one thing, but a working ship like *Endurance* also needs large amounts of electrical power, both to drive the various systems and equipment vital to the work of the ship and to provide domestic supplies for the crew in their living spaces. Each main diesel has a power take-off before the main gearbox, which drives the two shaft generators. These units produce enough electrical power to operate the ship and can still be driven even when the main engines are de-clutched and the screw still.

Besides the shaft generators, *Endurance* has two diesel-powered auxiliary generators driven independently from the main engines. One or both of these can be started when one of the main engines is de-clutched, as running the generators is more economical than using a main diesel just to create electricity. The auxiliaries are also used when the ship needs all of her engine output to drive the screw, or when she is alongside (in harbour) with the engines shut down.

Other systems include hydraulics which are used to operate: watertight doors, hatches, the anchors, and the cranes and davits that launch and retrieve the ship's boats. A Parat boiler provides steam for the heating system and the fresh water generators.

Other machinery spaces

Any ship is a complex mechanical device and *Endurance* is no exception. Throughout her hull there are many machinery spaces for the myriad of systems and equipment essential to her continued operation. For example, propulsion spaces include the shaft space, the steering gear compartment and the bow and stern thruster compartments. Then there are compartments for hydraulic systems, the incinerator and the diesel-driven fire pumps. And, of course, the engineers also have to look after the miles of pipework, conduit and cabling that extend throughout her hull.

Other spaces include the four Heating, Ventilation and Air Conditioning (HVAC) compartments from where air is pulled into the ship and distributed throughout as needed. This air can either be heated with steam or cooled with chilled water. *Endurance* was designed from the start for ice operations so has an extremely effective heating system. She was also originally designed for a much smaller complement so her air-conditioning, while upgraded, struggles when she transits through warmer equatorial and tropical waters.

Chapter Three - The Plum

The engineering department have the use of two workshops for essential maintenance and repairs. One is equipped with an array of bench and fixed power tools, and is used for mechanical engineering tasks. Components can be repaired, altered or in some cases rebuilt. The other workshop is the Electrical Maintenance Room (EMR), where the ship's electrical devices (those that can be moved there anyway) are maintained, adjusted and repaired.

A crew of 120 plus 20 or so passengers can get through a lot of fresh water when washing, cooking, and drinking. Fortunately, *Endurance* is equipped with two water generators that produce up to 50 tonnes of fresh water per day. These are steam-driven heaters that boil seawater into vapour, leaving the salt behind. This water vapour is then cooled and condensed as fresh water.

Bridge

If the engine room is the heart, then the bridge is surely the brain. And this ship has a big one. Her beam and her boxy superstructure allow a wide, spacious bridge, closer in size to that of an aircraft carrier than a ship of this tonnage.

In the centre of the bridge is where the watchkeepers and the helm work, and where the Officer of the Watch manages the ship. Steering is controlled from here, as are the engine speeds, propeller settings and various propulsion modes. But anyone expecting a large, spoked wooden wheel, speaking tubes and brass quadrants for ringing signal bells in the engine room will be disappointed. Instead there is an array of neat computer displays, control panels, small panel-mounted quadrant levers and telephone-style handsets. But at least there is still a high pedestal-mounted 'Captain's chair' in the centre.

The bridge also has repeater displays for the navigation and search radars. *Endurance* has five: three Bridgemaster E ARPA radars for anti-collision (including one mounted Ice radar on the bow) and two Type 1007 (I band) for navigation and aircraft control. She also has a range of radio and satellite communication systems that are mainly controlled from the separate communications room at the rear of the bridge.

To the port side is a planning station and is where the Navigator works. Large chart tables and storage drawers hold all the charts needed for a deployment, although as with many Royal Navy ships, paper charts are due to be replaced with digital versions, viewed through large screens. The advantages are many: chart updates are easier, you can zoom in and out to different levels of magnification, and various overlays can be attached to show particular information. But of course, should you have a computer or electrical failure you'll be quickly searching through the chart drawers once more.

A control and monitoring station for the sonar and survey gear is also placed on this side. When the ship is running a survey a watchkeeper monitors the equipment from here, starting and stopping the survey lines and the logging of data, while taking measurements of water temperature, wind, air temperature and other meteorological information.

On the starboard side of the bridge a large display board shows a schematic diagram of the ship complete with warning lights to help identify the location of fire alerts. In an emergency damage control and fire-fighting operations would be controlled from here.

And this side is also where 'the voice of the ship' works. The microphone and controls for the ship-wide tannoy system ('pipes' in Naval parlance) are used by a watchkeeper to pass on important information, warnings and all the other messages the crew need to hear.

Other workspaces

Other workspaces are placed throughout the ship, including the survey office, the armoury and various offices. At first glance most of these might look like any other small offices, with calendars and charts on the walls, files on shelves and a computers and trays on the desks. But you then notice the metal walls, thick windows (sometimes round), tidy locked cupboards and drawers with locked doors, and the laptop computer clamped to the desk. Not many offices need to be prepared for the pitching, rolling and shaking which occurs when a force eight gale blows up.

Hangar

One of the most powerful tools in *Endurance's* armoury is her aviation group, who operate two Westland Lynx helicopters from the large hangar at the rear of the superstructure. The Lynx has been the Royal Navy's tactical shipborne helicopter for over 25 years, serving in various forms and in a multitude of roles, such as anti-shipping, anti-submarine warfare, tactical support and reconnaissance. *Endurance* has two Mk 3 Lynx, and while they don't have the full range of combat equipment of their more warlike counterparts, they are reliable, tough and effective transports. Each has two gas turbine engines for safety and carries a cockpit crew of two. The rear compartment can hold up to nine people or a mixture of equipment, cargo or passengers. The Lynx is remarkably agile and powerful, yet by folding back the main rotor blades and the tail two of them can be rolled into *Endurance's* hangar.

Chapter Three - The Plum

When both aircraft are inside there is just enough space left for the maintenance crew to work on them. A high walkway around the side of the hangar gives access to various stores and equipment, including pre-packed safety rucksacks ('Bergens') for teams going ashore in the uninhabited ice and tundra. A nearby and separate aviation control room is where flying missions are planned and where the aviation group is run from.

The main hangar door rolls up to allow the aircraft to be moved out onto the open flight deck. This deck seems large when you walk across it – less so when trying to land on it at night, in high winds, in rain or snow, and with the ship pitching, rolling and heaving. In the middle of this deck is a grille-like grating. When the Lynx makes contact with the deck, a 'deck harpoon' beneath the fuselage can be hooked on to this grille, securing the aircraft to the ship even when she is rolling heavily. Various tie down points enable a helicopter to be made secure on deck once its engines are shut down.

The hold

Endurance has the role of supporting scientific and survey expeditions and various isolated communities in the South Atlantic and Antarctic. To fulfil this she usually has to transport quantities of specialised equipment, supplies and survival gear. Less usual deliveries include items such as building materials. Up to 270 tonnes of stores can be carried in her main hold, under the forward deck. When the ship is preparing to leave the UK on her annual deployment, this hold is crammed full of containers, each one carrying equipment and other stores, either for the ship or for one of her customer organisations. Packing them in the correct order for access when needed is an art in itself. Containers are usually stacked to two levels and a high walkway around the hold gives access to the top layer.

Living spaces

Endurance's crew is nominally 120 strong, but she usually has extra guests on board, such as British Antarctic Survey scientists, film crews, specialist expeditions and even publishers. But compared to most other Royal Navy ships, her accommodation is spacious and comfortable and with plentiful access to windows. Most crew members share two or three to a cabin, with a good quantity of locker space and drawers. This doesn't sound much – until you compare it to what's available in a frigate or destroyer. *Endurance* even has carpets! Heads of Department have the luxury of a cabin to themselves, while the Captain has a small suite, with a sleeping cabin and adjacent office.

Junior rates Mess laid out for Valentine's supper

Officers Ward Room

NAFFI Stores

CHAPTER THREE - **The Plum**

Junior ranks can meet, eat or socialise in their large mess with its TV, food servery and vending machines. Petty officers have their own mess, while the commissioned officers have the wardroom. This runs the width of the ship and is directly beneath the bridge, with an array of large picture windows giving dramatic views over the forward deck. A separate officers dining room is adjacent, complete with light wooden panelling and with maritime prints and photographs on the walls.

Other living spaces include the ship's laundry – an essential feature when so many people are living and working so close together for so long. And *Endurance* even has a library, where crew members can peruse a selection of books or study quietly for exams.

Meals for all ranks are prepared in the galley, which to the uninitiated, looks like a typical commercial kitchen. Which is why it's unusual. Popular with the catering team it's much more spacious (and they say, better-designed,) than those on warships of comparable size.

Ship's boats

Endurance is well equipped with seven boats, including rigid, semi-rigid and inflatable types. Five boats carry out transport and general work, and two of them, the *Stancomb Wills* and the *Dudley Docker*, are named after the lifeboats used by Shackleton's Endurance expedition. The Captain's launch is named *Eddie Shackleton*.

But there are also two specialist boats unique to the role of this ship. Survey Motor Boat (SMB) *Nimrod* and SMB *James Caird* are in the 9 tonne class, and are fitted with echo sounding equipment and GPS navigation gear. *Nimrod* is named after the ship used by Shackleton's 1907 expedition, while the original *James Caird* was the lifeboat used by Shackleton in his epic 1916 sea crossing from Elephant Island to South Georgia. The SMBs can independently carry out coastal hydrographic and mapping tasks, often in areas too restricted for *Endurance* herself. They greatly increase the ship's survey capacity and allow many more tasks to be completed than can be handled by a single hull.

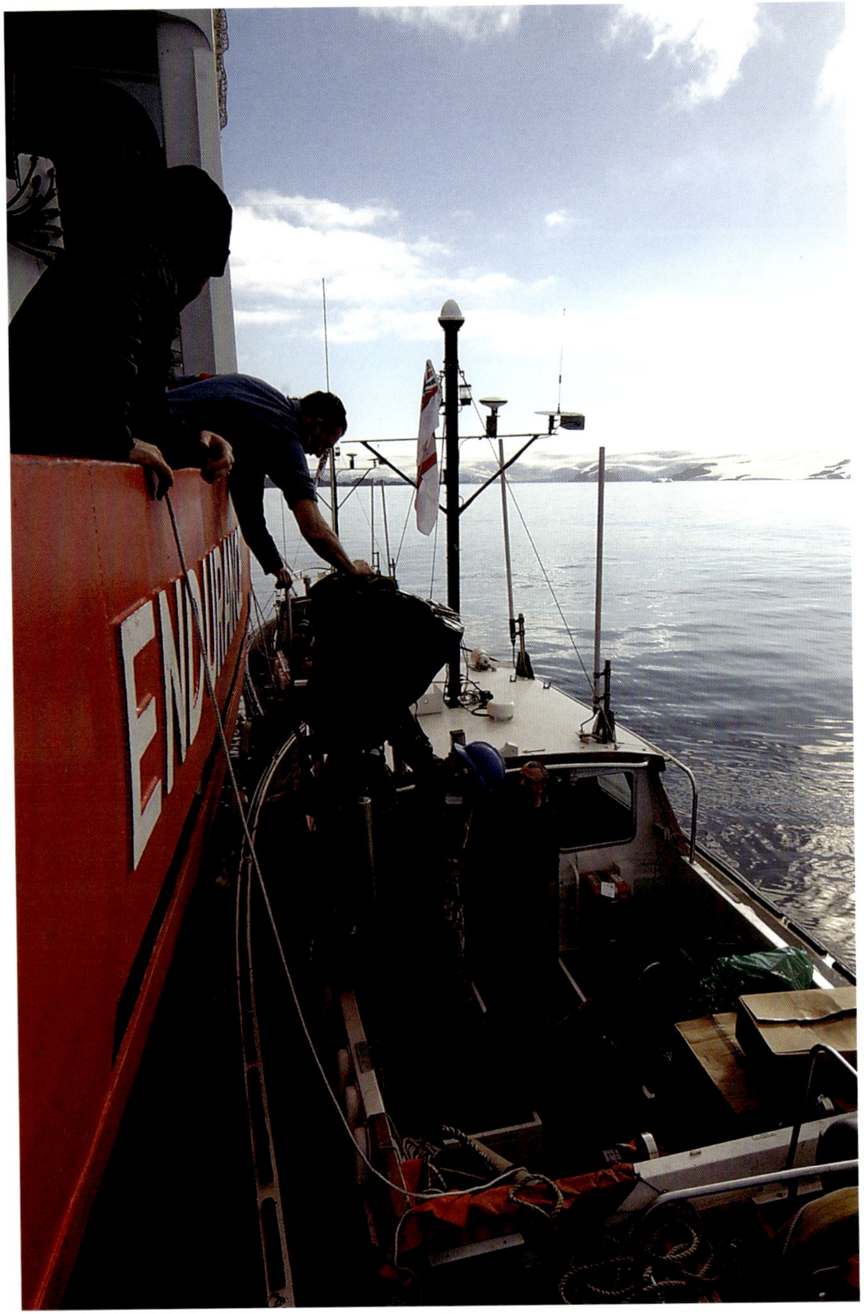

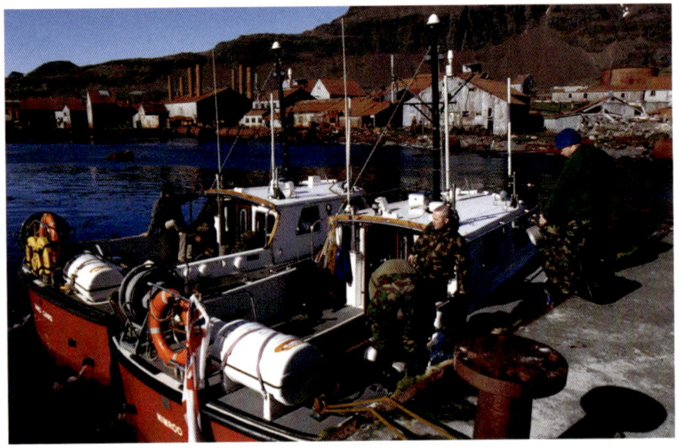

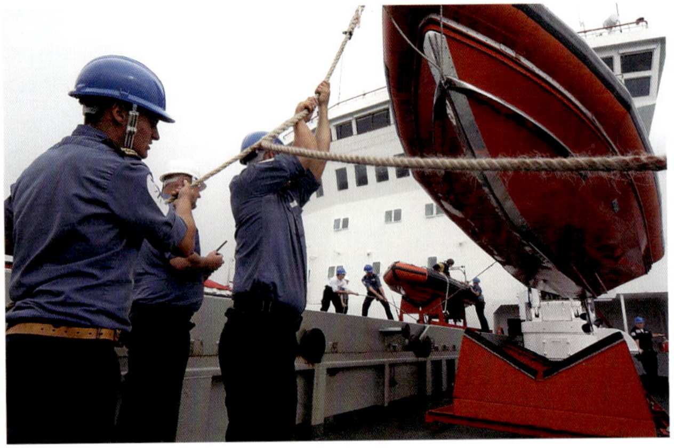

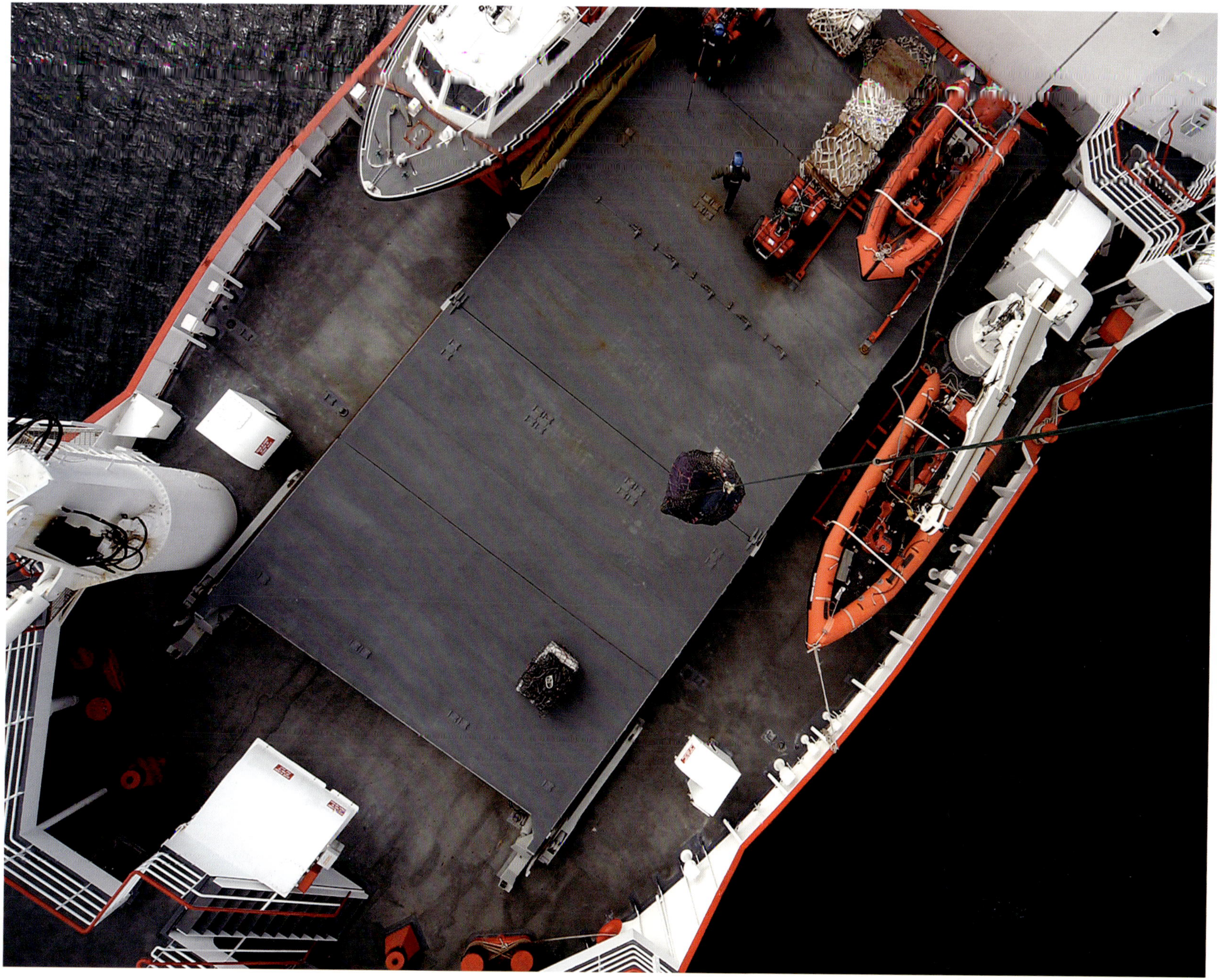

Chapter Four

Endurance at Work

She may not look it, but *Endurance* is most definitely a vessel of the Royal Navy. Her crew are Navy and she follows naval routines and procedures. Her role is unique however, and because of this, and because she sails to such distant and uninhabited places, she is regarded as a desirable posting. Many volunteer for drafts to her, and those lucky enough to serve on her usually regard their Antarctic journey as a highlight of their career.

The Royal Navy is an integrated service, and about one in five of all new entrants are now women. Women and men serve alongside each other in all the Navy's surface ships, and *Endurance* is no exception. And as with any other service unit, the make-up of her complement isn't static. Crew members come and go regularly, and on each deployment time is spent blending new joiners and existing crew into an efficient team.

As with other ships, everyone has more than one job. So while the Regulatory Petty Officer may have ship's discipline and policing as his or her core duty, they may also be a Flight Deck Officer, responsible for the safe launching and retrieval of helicopters. The Leading Chef is a key member of the fire-fighting team, while a logistics officer may have education and personal development responsibilities for the whole crew.

Crew members also have to pitch in during seamanship evolutions such as berthing or deploying or recovering boats. And of course there are countless daily maintenance tasks which need to be done, such as cleaning rust on the hull and superstructure, greasing winches and fittings and keeping the paintwork in trim. 'It's not my job' is not a statement that gets any sympathy or consideration in today's Navy!

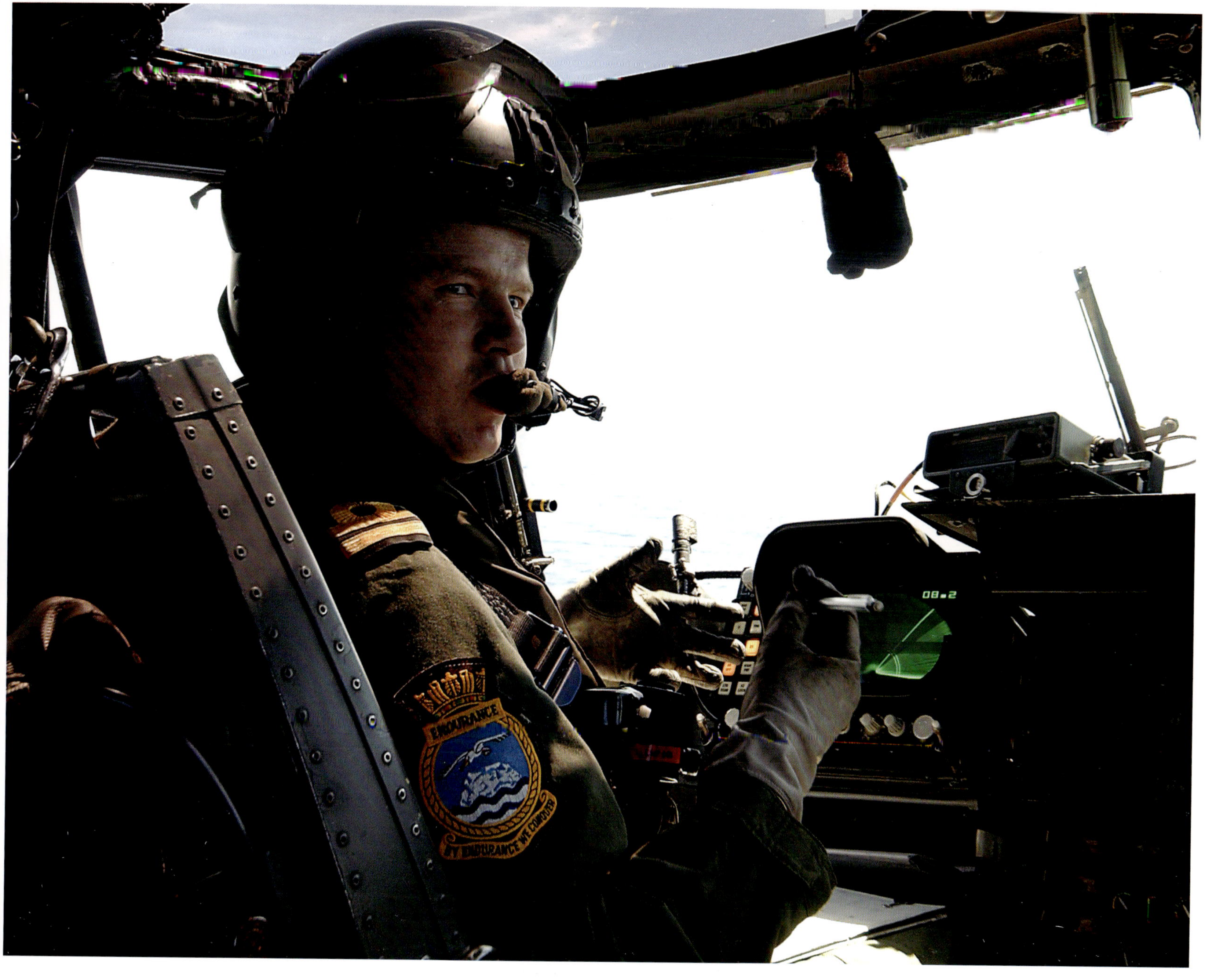
ENDURANCE
BY ENDURANCE WE CONQUER
08.2

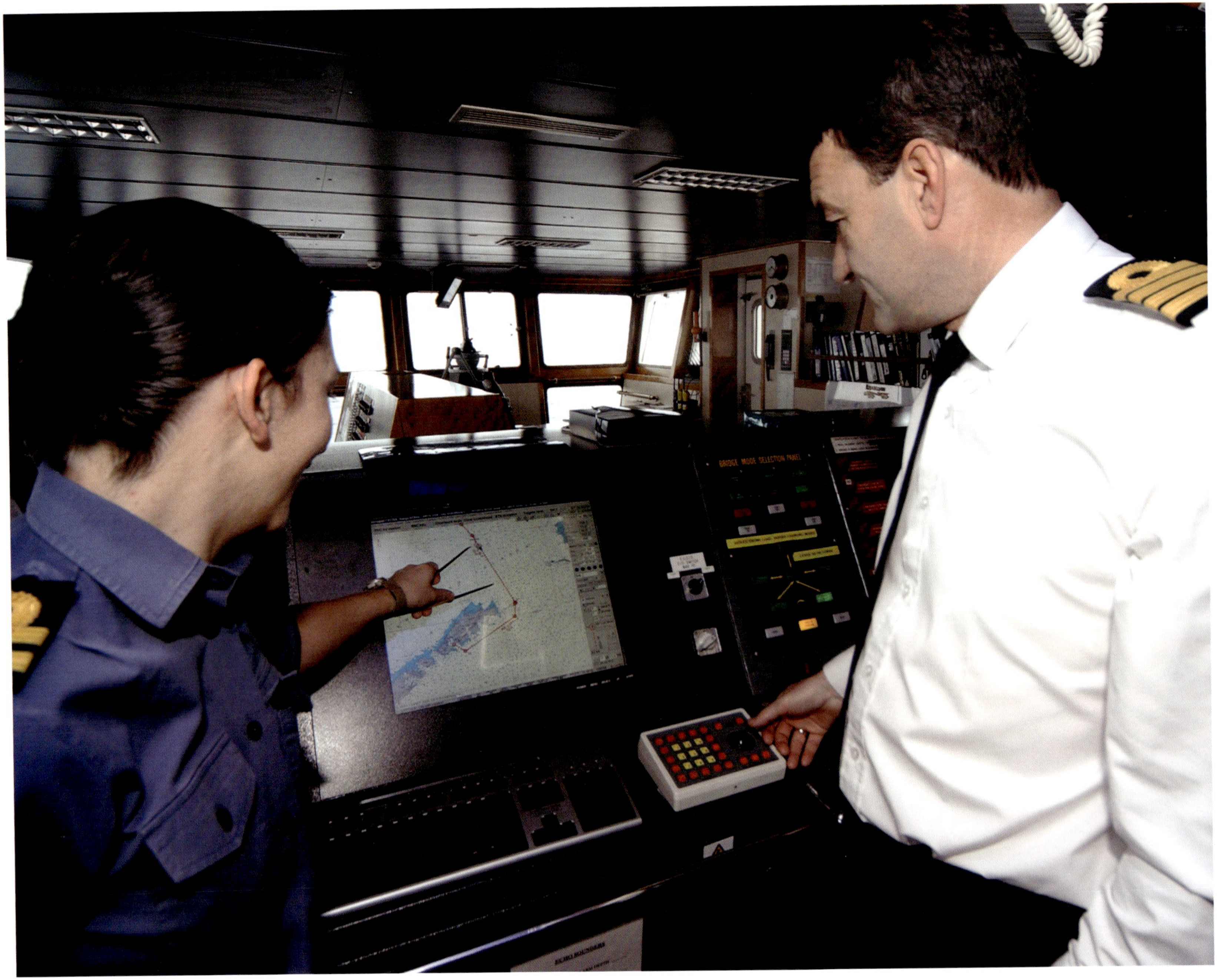
BRIDGE MODE SELECTION PANEL

Chapter Four - Endurance at Work

Command

Endurance has probably more independence than any other Royal Navy ship of similar size. She may not lead a task group, but she does operate on her own, at huge distances from any support. And so her Commanding Officer is a full Captain, wearing four rings on his sleeve – an unusually senior rank for a single ship of this size. Command of *Endurance* is a sought-after posting, with Officers enjoying both the independence and responsibility while valuing the opportunity to travel to lonely and wild places that few of us ever get the chance to see.

The Captain has final responsibility for the operation of *Endurance*, for carrying out the tasks assigned to her, and for the safety of the ship, her helicopters and her crew. He or she has the ability to communicate with Fleet Headquarters in the UK, and can get advice or instructions quicker and easier previous Captains. The Captain also has the Executive Officer and a senior command team to manage the ship and its day-to-day operations, and to provide advice where needed. But in the end the Captain is still the commander on the spot, encouraged by naval tradition, culture and training to exercise independent judgement – and of course, to take the responsibility for the outcome.

The ship is organised into various functional departments, each with an Officer at its head. These Heads of Department plan each day's activities; with the overall target of achieving all the tasks in the work plan agreed with the various stakeholder and 'customer' groups before leaving the UK. In drawing up the detailed daily plan they have to take into account factors such as the weather and sea state, ice predictions, the current operational state of ship and her equipment, the state of her crew and the sometimes conflicting priorities of the different stakeholders.

By the very nature of the work and the environment, schedules must remain fluid. If *Endurance* faces extended periods of bad weather, problems with equipment or any other unplanned events, the command team may need to prioritise tasks and even set some aside for a subsequent deployment.

While the ship operates continually and some roles demand constant 'watches' for 24 hours a day, most of the ship's complement follow a 'working day' routine. Crew members are usually up early, anything from 5.30 onwards. The structure of every working day is set by Daily Orders: the list of planned events or 'serials' which details and timetables all the tasks for that day. The first flights and boat launches are usually at 09.00, and these operations will run through until about 17.00. In theory most of the crew have free time after the evening meal and at weekends. But, of course, if the work demands they will put in many more hours -- and if the whole ship needs to run a 24-hour watch cycle then she does.

Chapter Four - Endurance at Work

Executive department

The smooth running of the ship depends on the various departments working together in a jigsaw of responsibilities and roles. And it's the Executive Officer (XO) who has the job of making this work. Known as the 'Jimmy' in naval slang, he or she is second in command, and effectively the eyes, ears and hands of the Captain.

Every day at sea there is an evening Command Briefing. But before then, the XO holds a pre-brief co-ordination meeting with the Heads of Department. Departments often compete for resources and priority and it's the XO's role to balance these needs to best achieve the ship's mission. This command team then present the agreed plan at the Command Brief at 18.00, where the Heads of Department report to the Captain on the status of their responsibilities. Sometimes the Captain has to decide between a series of options presented by the command team, but as a good XO must be completely aware of the Captain's own priorities, such situations should be rare.

At the end of the Command Brief, the Daily Orders for the following day are finalised. And at 08.00 the following day, the Heads of Department attend the daily Operation Brief, where they review the weather, the ship's status and the day's plan.

Discipline

Maintenance of discipline is important in any service community, but perhaps especially so in the confines of a Royal Navy ship. *Endurance* has no police force as such and all in the chain of command, from the Captain down, have a responsibility to ensure the orderly running of the ship and conformance to Naval Regulations. However, the Executive Department has direct remit for this, and has the nearest thing to a ship's police officer in the shape of the Regulatory Petty Officer (RPO). The RPO provides advice and support on regulatory and policing issues, and where necessary, enforcement. Significant infractions are rare, and most of the RPO's time is spent in an advisory role, rather like a land-based Community Policeman. Of course, along with everyone else onboard, the RPO has other roles to carry out, including delivering the ship's post, and acting as a Flight Deck Officer when helicopter flying is taking place.

Seamanship

Specialist trades notwithstanding, every member of the Royal Navy is trained in basic seamanship skills and in the practicalities of

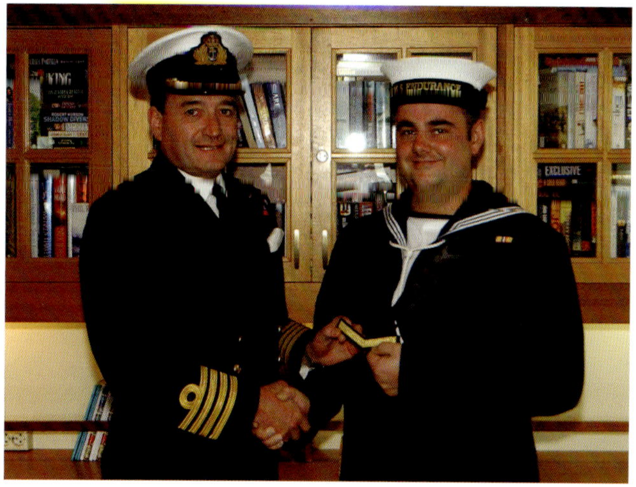
EXCLUSIVE

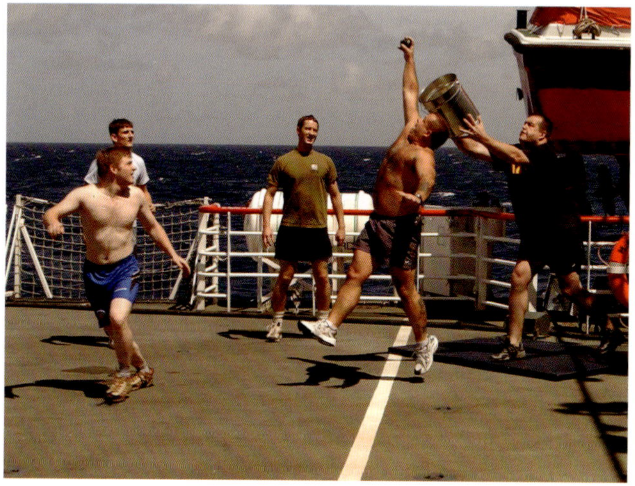

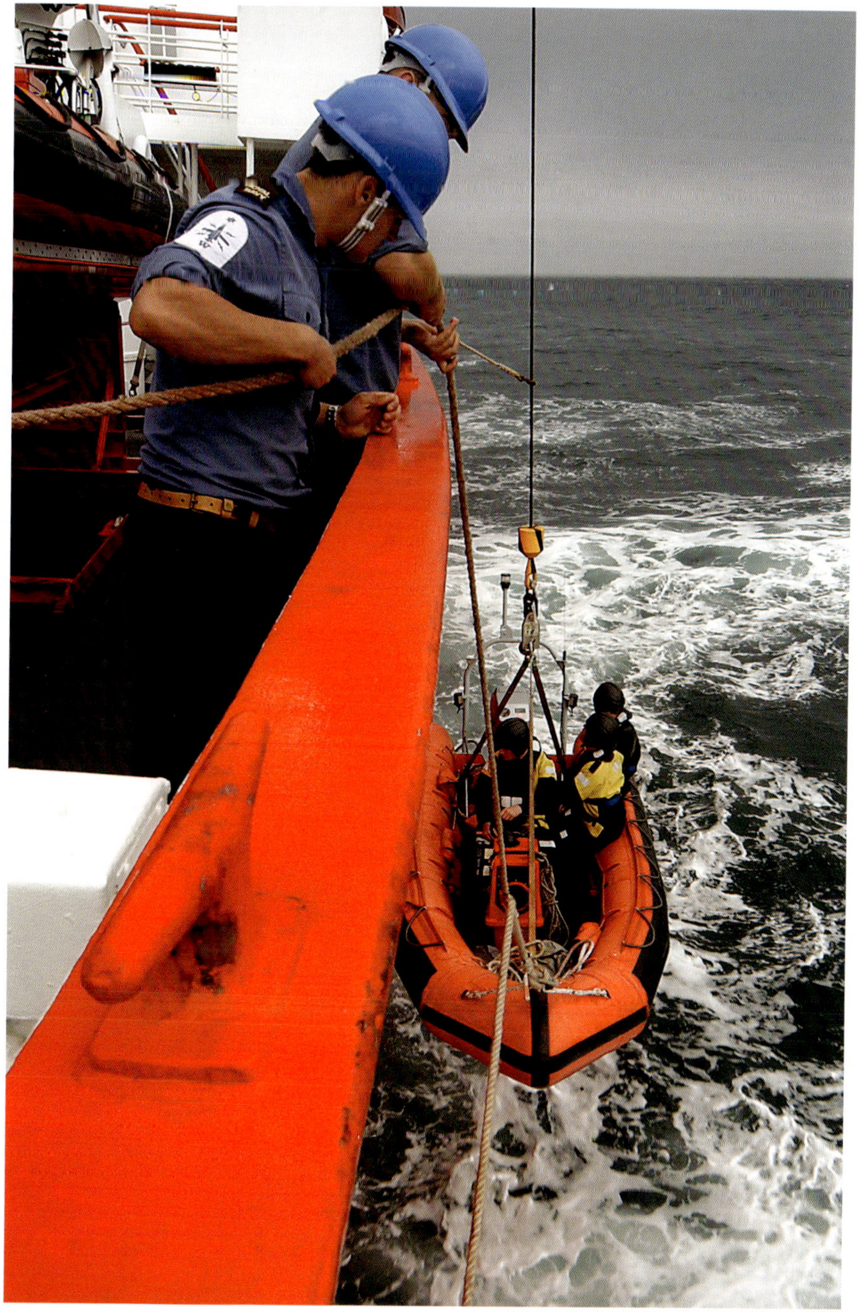

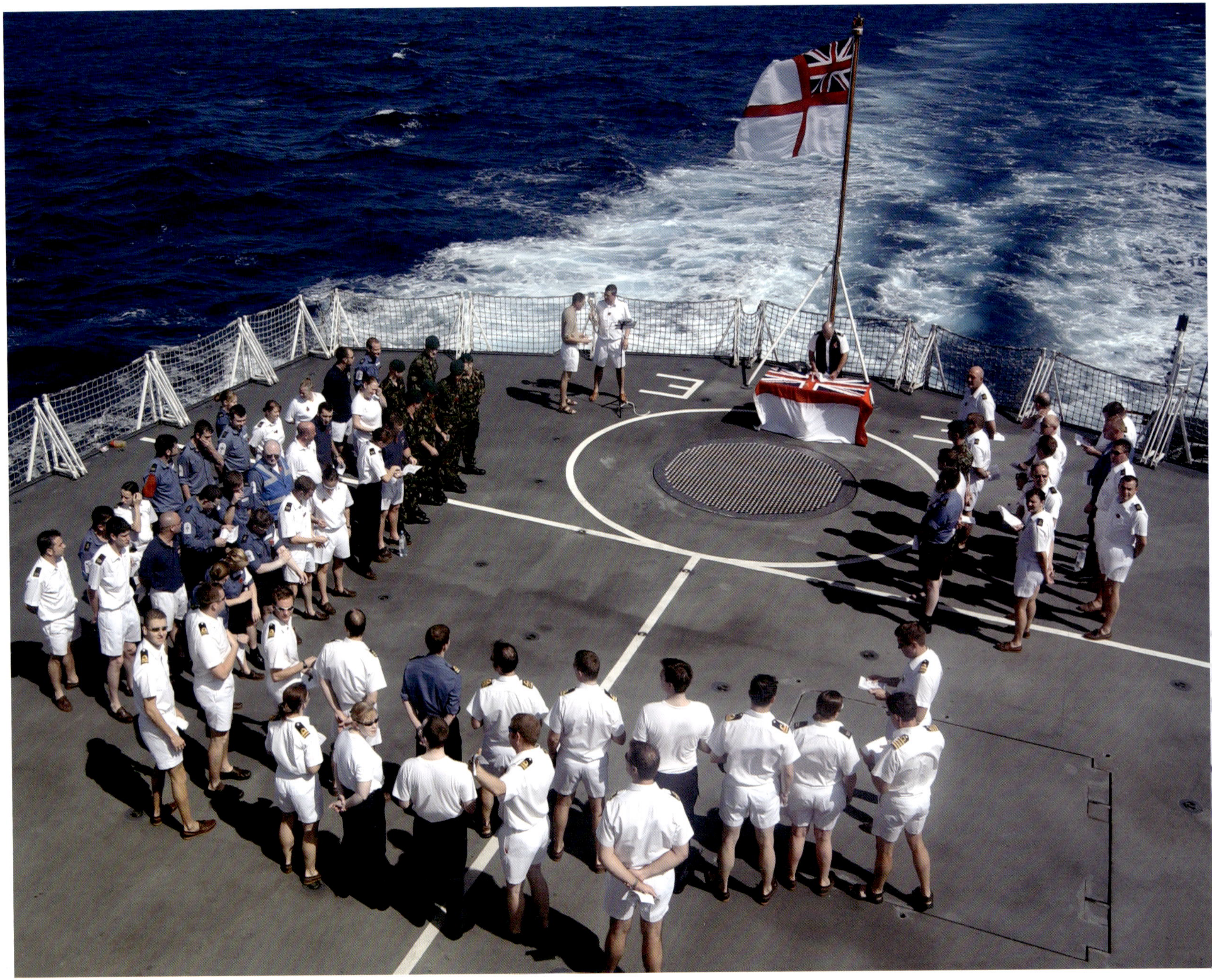

Chapter Four - Endurance at Work

operating a ship at sea. Evolutions such as coming alongside or sailing, dropping and raising anchor or launching and retrieving boats all need manpower (or womanpower) to carry them out. The Executive Department, with the Chief Bosun's Mate (known as the 'Buffer') and their team, provide the specialist skills for these operations and relevant training for others of the ship's company who need to help out. And it's not just these particular operations that the crew need to take part in. A ship at sea is continually attacked by the elements, and needs continual and regular attention to prevent corrosion and general deterioration of exposed surfaces. The cleaning, maintenance and preservation of external surfaces and equipment are vital tasks that are co-ordinated by the Buffer and his or her team.

Fitness

A healthy, fit crew is essential to meet the rigours of naval life, so most vessels have a Physical Training Instructor (PTI). Working within the Executive Department and inevitably nicknamed 'Clubz', from the days when much of the exercises involved swinging large clubs around, the PTI provides training, encouragement and 'persuasion' for all members of the ship's complement. *Endurance* has a remarkably well-equipped gym which is heavily used by the crew, while the PTI also runs regular circuit-training sessions and workouts on the flight deck. He or she also arranges plenty of sporting contests in various disciplines, both within the ship and against other ships and teams from the places *Endurance* visits.

And the PTI also provides individual training and help for those who might have difficulty passing the Navy's annual fitness test. It's noticeable that at the end of a deployment when *Endurance* is sailing home, the PTI's trade increases as crew members try to tone themselves up and sometimes lose some weight before they return to their families.

Warfare department

Even though *Endurance* has no weapons and doesn't have a specific warfighting role, she still has a Warfare Department. Led by the Operations Officer, this department in effect manages the operations of the ship, including those of the bridge team, navigation, communications and the small Royal Marines detachment.

Bridge team

At all times there is an Officer of the Watch on the bridge, with direct minute-by-minute responsibility for the safety of ship and crew. A

Chapter Four - Endurance at Work

pattern of watches (or shifts) ensures that there is someone on duty in this position 24 hours a day while at sea. They are usually one of the ship's experienced officers but can also be a junior officer under supervision who is being trained for the role. The Officer of the Watch in effect commands the ship whilst they are on duty although the Captain can take over at any time he or she sees fit. Working closely with the rest of the bridge team, the Officer of the Watch supervises the ship's operations, her route and speed, propulsion modes, the deployment and retrieval of boats, flight operations, and all the other actions that are going on. This can be particularly challenging if *Endurance* is operating inshore, perhaps close to a dangerous, unmapped coastline, maybe inside an uncharted bay with a jagged rocky inlet, or perhaps trying to thread her way into a crowded harbour. And, of course, the challenge is increased when weather, sea or ice conditions make things more difficult.

Before deployment, bridge personnel attend training courses at HMS *Collingwood*, the Hampshire base which houses two computer-driven Bridge Training simulators. Here they deal with different scenarios and problems, refreshing their skills and ensuring their teamwork and procedures are effective. And immediately before deployment the bridge team are put through their paces during the Operational Sea Training (OST) exercises.

Endurance's bridge team are unusual within the Navy as they need to regularly deal with ice operations. The training for this is handled by the Operations Officer during the programme run once *Endurance* has set sail. And two RN officers each year also attend an annual International Ice Operations course hosted in Argentina, a course which helps share knowledge and best practice between all the services that send ships into these hostile waters.

Steering the ship

Endurance travels much of the time with the steering set to automatic, where a computerised system keeps her on the planned course and desired speed. But when complex manoeuvring is called for one of the bridge team takes the helm, and becomes the nearest person there is to the ship's 'driver'. They may steer *Endurance*, but they do so while being commanded by the Officer of the Watch, who also sets the engine controls and the speed. *Endurance's* propulsion system is flexible and can easily be reconfigured to suit different operating regimes. When the ship is in transit or operating normally, she usually has one engine operating, clutched into the gearbox at 720 rpm. As well as transmitting motive power to the screw, this engine drives its shaft generator to provide electrical power to the ship. If more power is needed or higher speeds required the second engine is started and clutched in as well. When manoeuvring at low speed, say in a harbour or coastal inlet, some of the electrical power is diverted to the bow and stern thrusters for manoeuvring. And should it be necessary in an emergency, the engine, gearbox and propeller pitch can be operated in local mode, where they are controlled from the engine control room.

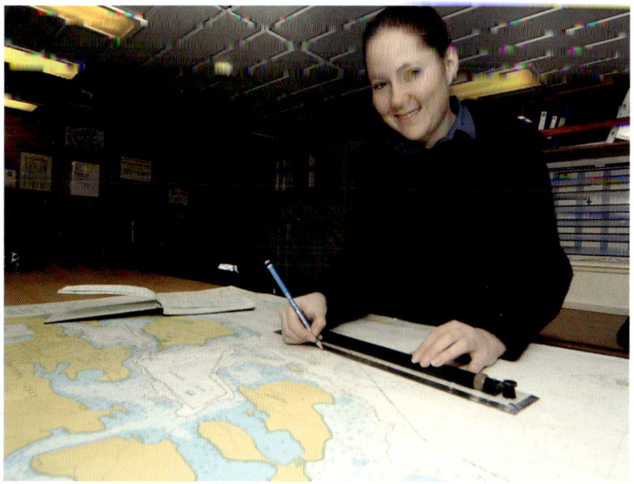

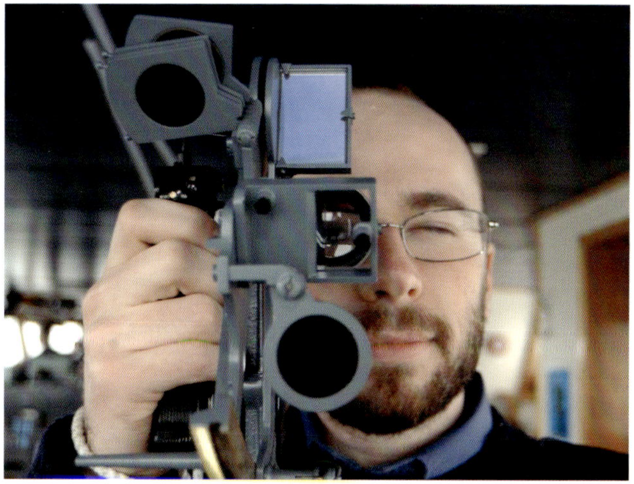

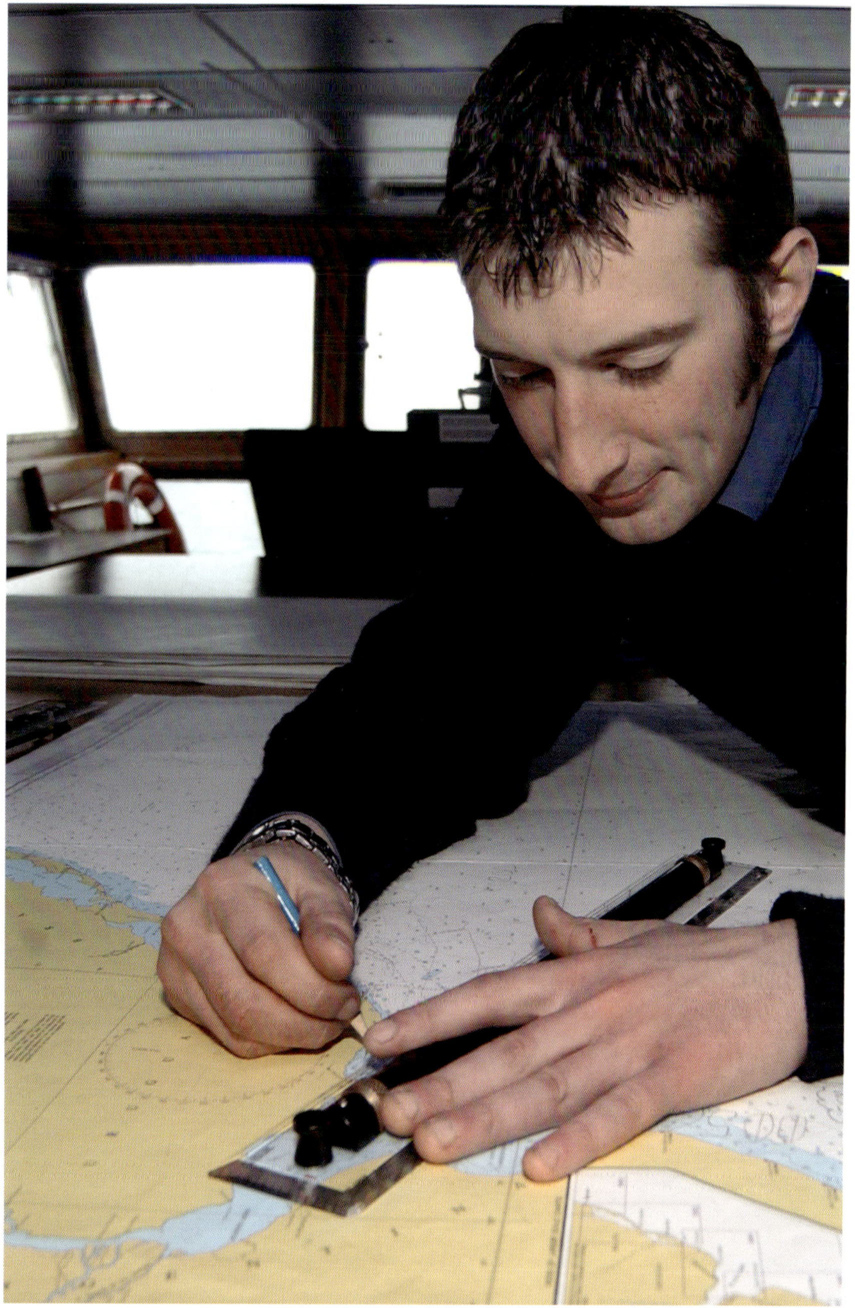

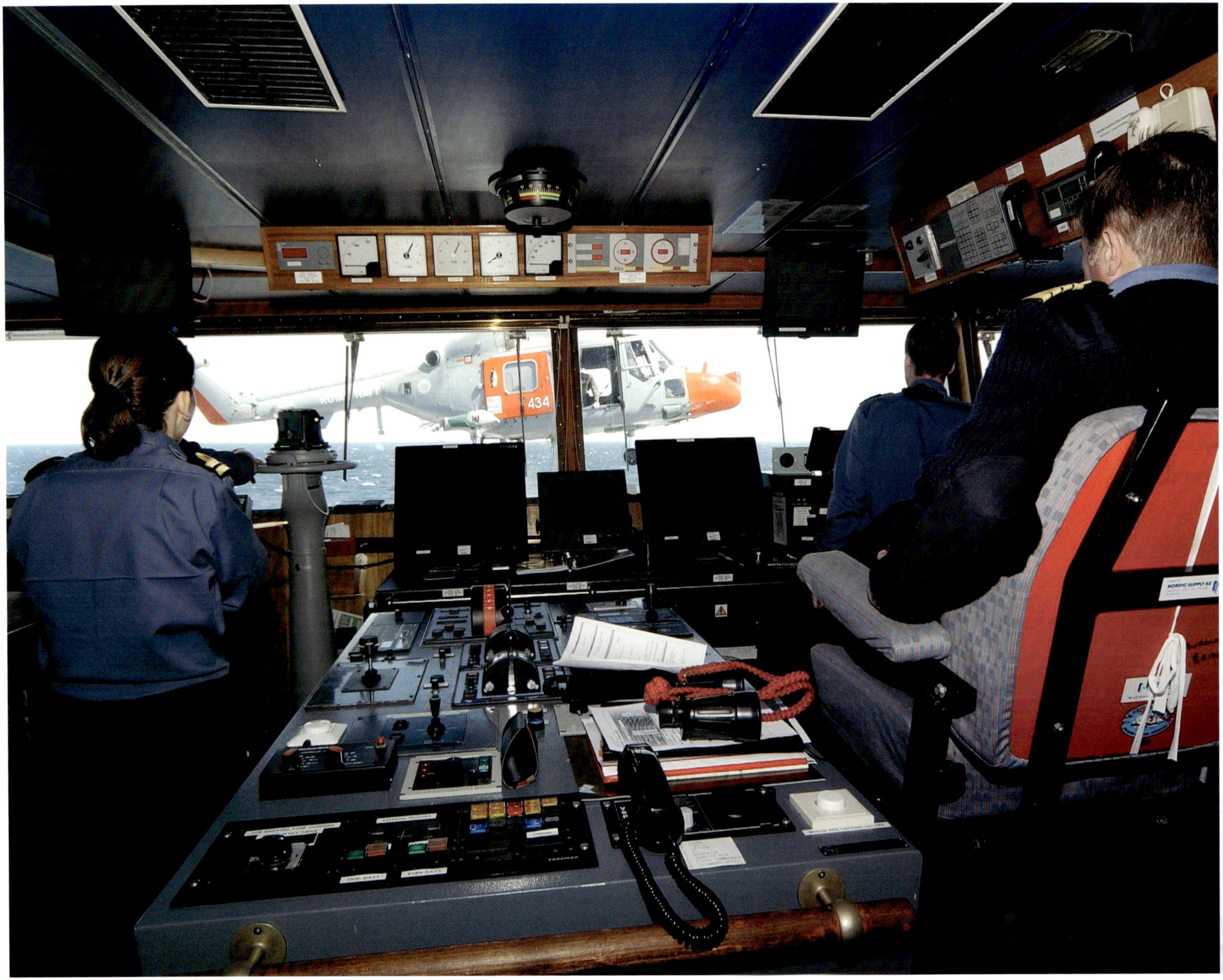
434
ODD DAYS
EVEN DAYS
NORDIC SUPPLY AS

CHAPTER FOUR - **Endurance at Work**

Endurance sometimes has to break through ice to continue her mission, although she doesn't so much break the ice as crush it. During ice-breaking both engines are clutched in and run at 750 rpm. To maximise the power going to the screw the shaft generators are disconnected and the auxiliary generators started for electrical power.

When she comes up against thick ice, the engine revs are built up as the bow is pushed forward. Her flat profile means that she starts to lift up onto the ice until her weight and the sharp blade edge beneath the bow cracks the ice open and the ship drops back down into the new channel she has created. Ice-breaking can be heard throughout the ship, as the engine revs build up and the ice scrapes and thump against the hull. And if the ship's approach angle is slightly off centre when she hits larger pieces the crew can feel the slight deflection as the bow is pushed to the side.

Endurance can safely break though up 1.5 m of first year ice. Ice that is older has been compressed by the weight of subsequent ice on top and has become almost transparent. This is much stronger and harder to break through.

Navigation

No ship can operate safely if the crew don't know where they are. *Endurance* works around some of the most dangerous coastlines and faces seas as rough as those anywhere in the world, so it is doubly essential for her to have a clear and accurate picture of her position. Every naval officer is trained in navigation techniques, although every ship also has one officer who has this as their main role and who is referred to as the 'Navigator'.

Endurance's Navigator uses a number of methods to fix her position. At sea, GPS satellite navigation is an important tool, although there are sometimes problems with satellite coverage. When closer to shore, radar is used to fix bearings and distance from identifiable landmarks. Inside visual range the Navigator can take bearings from headlands or identifiable points, while the water depth under the keel can be checked against the detailed depth soundings marked on the charts. And, of course, one of *Endurance's* prime roles is taking the very measurements that make these charts accurate and useful.

Traditional astro-navigation techniques are still available as a back-up to supplement the technology, where sightings are taken of the sun or stars, then the angles plotted and checked against pre-prepared tables of data to fix the ship's position. The Royal Navy is one of the few services that still teaches this technique to all trainee officers.

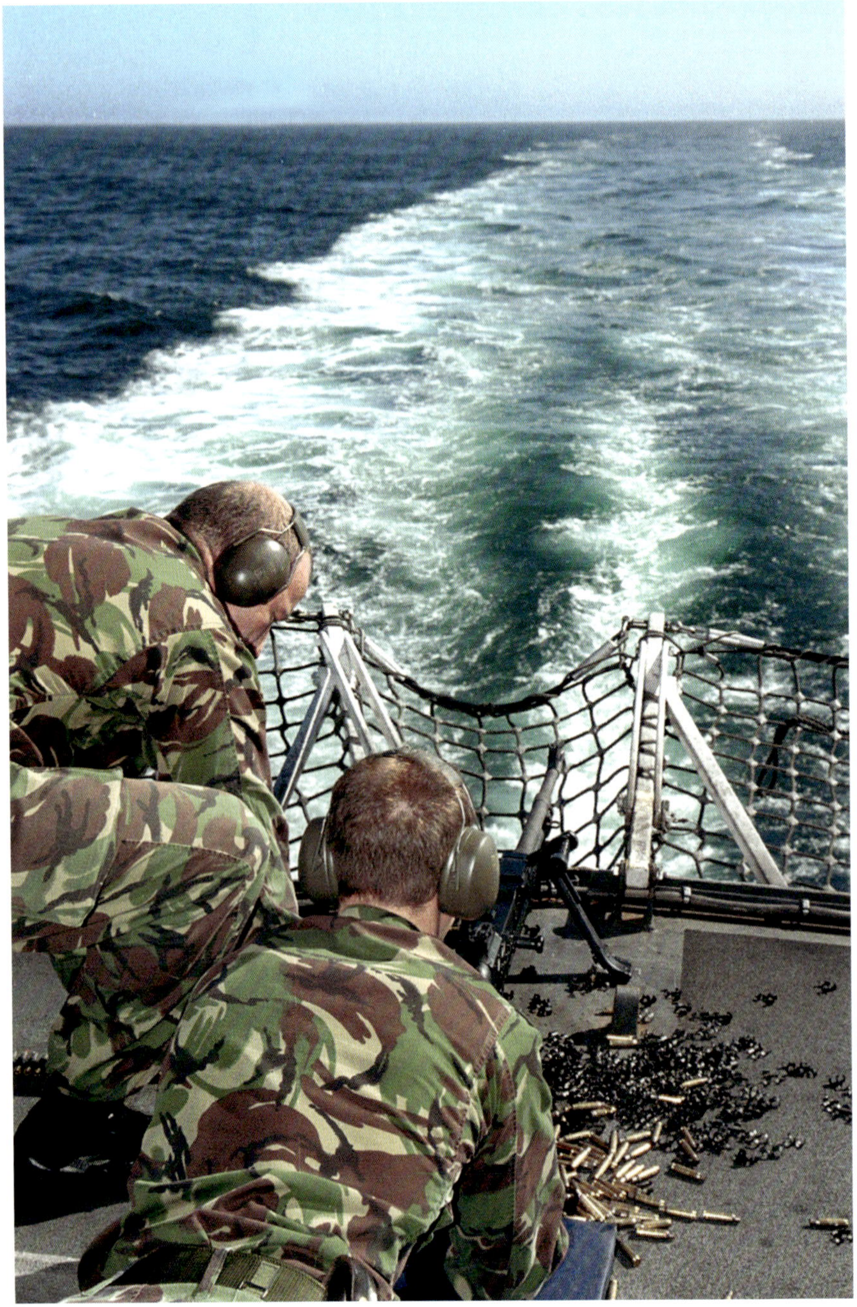

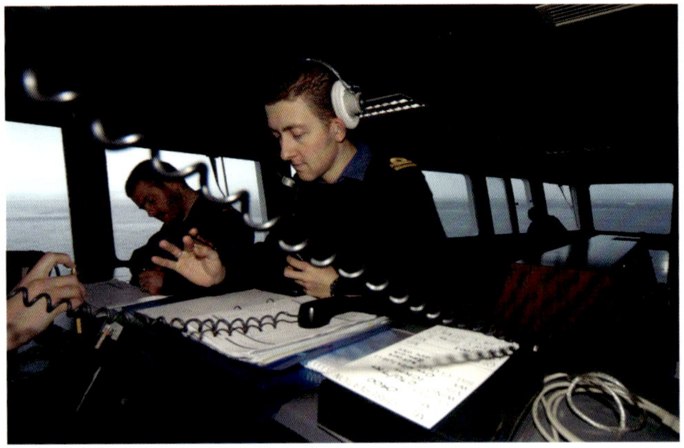

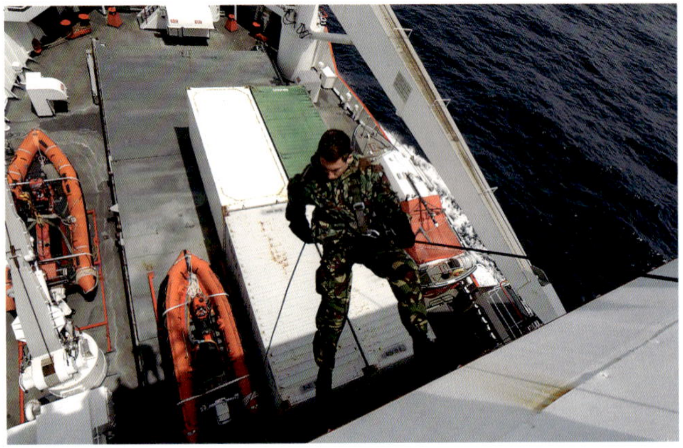

CHAPTER FOUR - **Endurance at Work**

Communications

Endurance is expected to operate on her own, hundreds of kilometres away from any support base. For her own safety, and as a unit of the Royal Navy, she needs to be able to communicate at great distances: with her headquarters in the UK, with other ships and with other agencies and bases in the Antarctic. The primary form of long-range communications for all Royal Navy vessels is still HF (High Frequency) radio. HF is very difficult to intercept or jam, although it is slow to transmit long messages and can be greatly affected by weather conditions, including the extreme cold that *Endurance* faces on a daily basis.

A more sophisticated but more expensive method is the satellite-based system known as INMARSAT. Available 24 hours a day, INMARSAT can send and receive telephone conversations, faxes and emails to and from anywhere in the world, in any weather conditions and whether or not the ship is rolling and pitching in rough seas. Up to a quarter of the ship's communications are personal messages. Each week every crew member is allowed 20 minutes of telephone time to talk to friends and relatives in the UK, while they also have access to computer terminals and email.

Local radio communications are essential to maintain the safety of her boats, aircraft and shore parties. When such a team is operating independently they will be given a schedule of times where they report their status by radio. Should a few of these scheduled slots be missed the ship will assume the shore or boat party has a problem and will begin emergency search and retrieval operations.

Marines

Endurance is an unarmed platform, although she does have a few rifles and machine guns for self-defence. There is also a six-man detachment of the Royal Marines on board. While they could take on defensive or warfighting tasks if needed, their primary job is to provide expertise in cold weather survival, mountaineering and arctic operations. Many Marines volunteer for this popular detachment, and all of those that are selected have completed ski survival and winter warfare courses.

One or two Marines are sent shore with every survey party or scientific team to provide advice and safety backup. At other times they practice their warfighting roles, or help train members of the ships company in weapons handling. And as the Antarctic treaty commits all the signatories to keeping the area a demilitarised zone, all weapons are locked away in the armoury once the ship travels below the Antarctic Circle.

Chapter Four - **Endurance at Work**

Engineering department

Most Royal Navy ships have two engineering departments, one dealing with propulsion and the ship's main systems, and the other maintaining weapons and related systems. *Endurance* is unusual in that she has a single Engineering Department that covers all aspects, although there is a Weapons Engineering specialist on board who deals with the survey and navigation equipment.

Within this single department there are eight sub-sections, each dealing with different aspects of the ship, including:

- ship's structure and ventilation
- engineering planning and logistics
- electrical control systems
- domestic electrics (galley, lighting, fire detection etc)
- engine room auxiliary systems
- engine room main engines
- outside machinery (boats, air conditioning, fridges)
- weapons, survey and navigation equipment

These individual roles and specialisations may be defined, but in practice the whole department works as a team, with the different sections helping each other to identify and fix any defects.

At any time there are two people on watch in the Engine Control Room, keeping an eye on system performance, looking out for problems and making sure the ship's command has motive power at all times. The rest of the team are usually working on scheduled maintenance or unplanned repairs to equipment that has failed ('emergent' maintenance). A computerised Maintenance Management System helps with scheduling and management of resources, although the workload varies considerably as things don't normally break down to a regular predictable schedule. Tasks can be as diverse as scheduled maintenance on the main engine, managing fuel transfer between the various tanks or fixing communications or electronic equipment. Domestic tasks could be unblocking a toilet or helping with personal electronics.

And constant training also takes place, with the team regularly practising the drills they use to deal with all kinds of system or machinery failure.

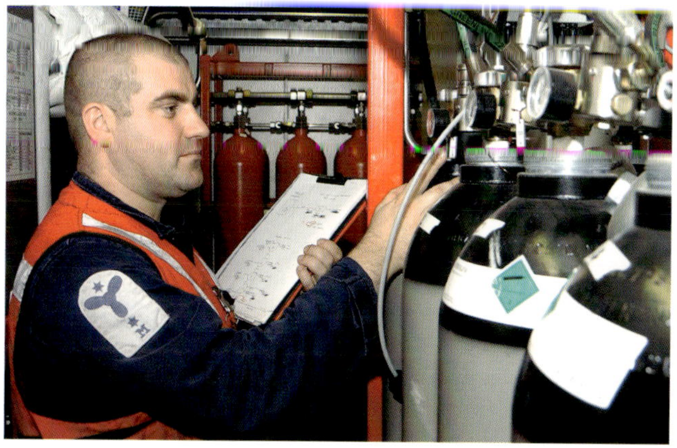

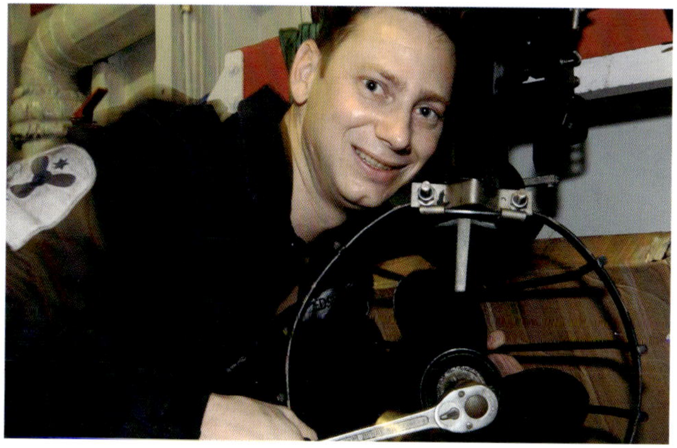

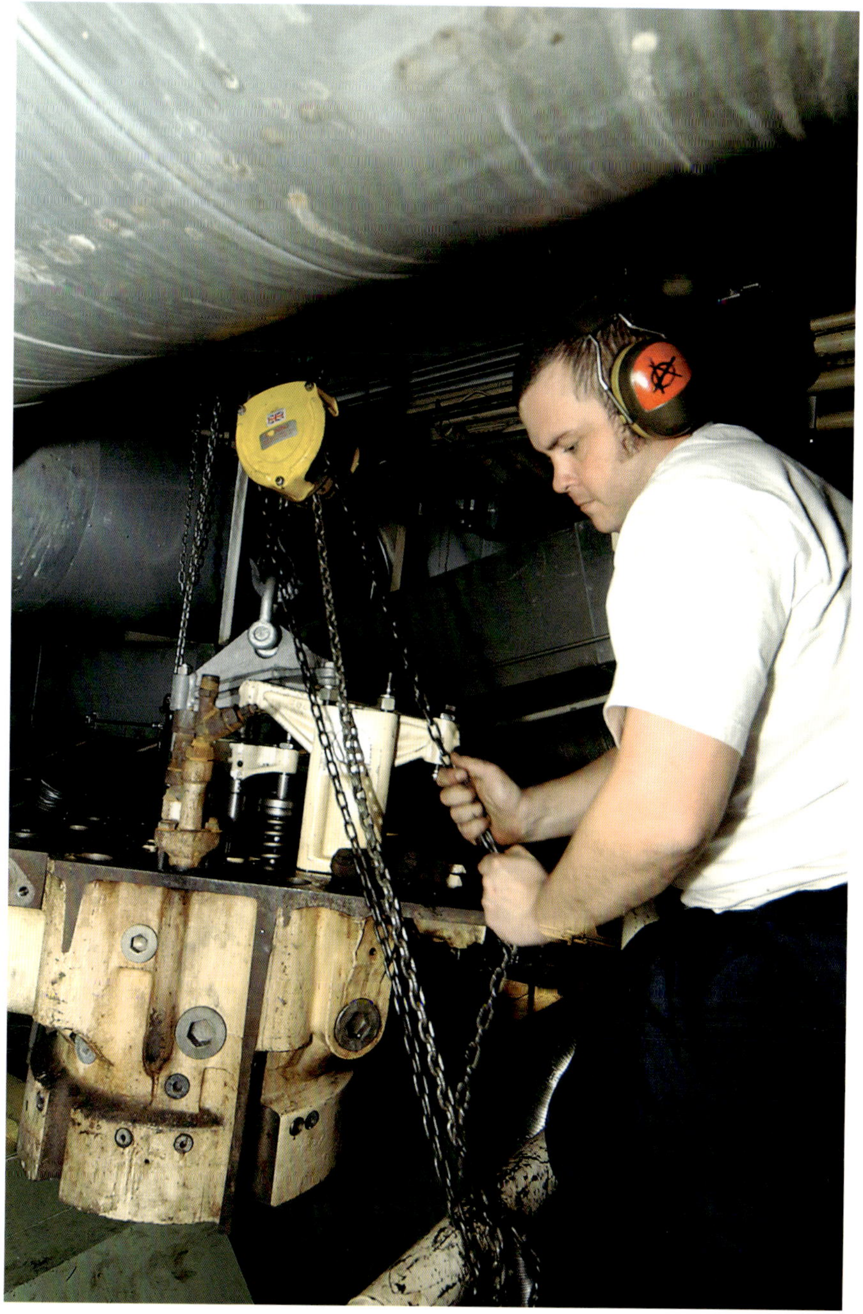

Chapter Four - Endurance at Work

Endurance has more than 15 years' service and her age means that defects are becoming more extensive and varied. She was also built to civilian standards so the engineering team don't have the same operating documentation as a grey warship. Spare parts are often not available within the normal Royal Navy supply chain and some need to be delivered from Norway. And the age of the ship means that some components are no longer available anyway. The unusual design of *Endurance* along with her independent role and the distance to her operating area means that self-reliance is the key. The engineering team will try to sort problems from their own resources, and are remarkably creative in coming up with solutions and work-arounds. Should spare parts be needed, the logistics team have a number of ways of getting them to the ship. More serious problems will be worked-around until Endurance can get access to dock facilities, often in South America.

A typical deployment will see *Endurance* moving from temperate weather conditions, through the tropics to the freezing Antarctic. Such changes in temperature and humidity have their effect on the ship's electrical, mechanical and electronic systems. And as with any complex machinery, some problems can occur after a major refit, where systems have been ripped out and replaced en masse.

A significant problem occurred on a recent deployment when it became noticeable that the ship would not steer in straight line when the rudder was set for straight ahead. Instead she would continually drift to starboard. The ship's divers investigated and found that the rudder had become misaligned. So *Endurance* headed for dry-dock at the Argentine port of Puerto Belgrano and repair teams were flown out from the UK to assist the Argentinean dock staff. It took six days of hard work and a good deal of support and assistance from the Argentine Navy to fix the misalignment, then another day for the ship to be refloated and refuelled before setting sail once more. Ship's machinery can be very temperamental after such a dry-docking so the engineering department had to monitor things very carefully for the first few days afterwards.

Some other recent problems include: contaminated fuel tanks, INMARSAT problems where weather fax information could not be received, and a host of minor niggles, such as relay failures. But as with all Navy engineering teams, *Endurance* personnel take these in their stride, relying on their extensive training and their very much 'can-do' attitude.

Survey department

In many ways the survey department and their equipment are one of the reasons for *Endurance's* existence. The department carries out hydrographic and oceanographic surveys, collects meteorological data, records wildlife and sea state information and also provides weather forecasting for the command team.

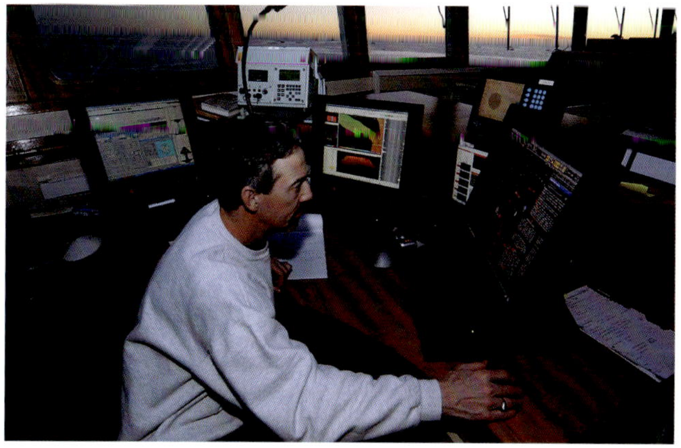

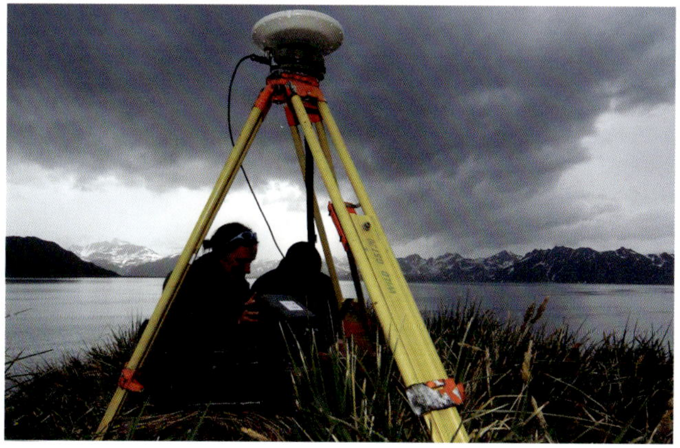

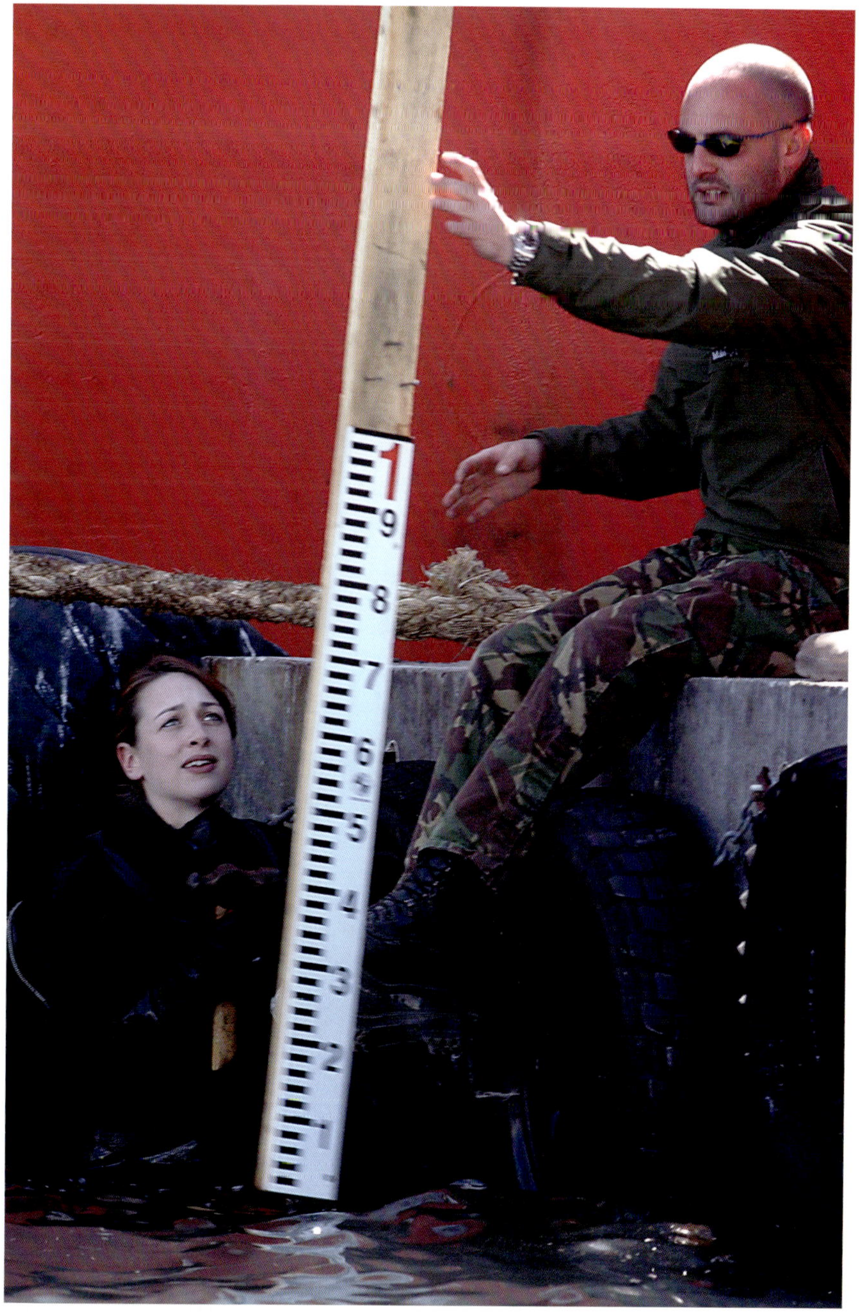

CHAPTER FOUR - **Endurance at Work**

Hydrographic survey

Some of the most important tasks carried out by *Endurance* are the surveys of the sea bottom and water depth in Antarctica. Carried out under the instructions of the UK Hydrographic Office (UKHO) they provide vital information for the creation or updating of maritime charts. In many of the places *Endurance* visits no accurate charts are available and her contribution is an important addition to maritime safety, especially as more and more tourist cruises are travelling to the Antarctic.

Endurance has some of the most sophisticated sensing and recording systems in the world. The main tools used to investigate the sea depth and sea bottom are echo sounders, where a pulse of sound is generated from a transducer in the ship's hull, then accurate measurements of the time taken for the sound reflected from the sea bottom come back to the ship. As the speed of sound through the sea is known, this time delay gives an accurate reading of the depth of the seabed. *Endurance's* single beam echo sounder can accurately read depths of up to 8000 m (26,250 ft), directly beneath the hull.

A more sophisticated sensor is her EM 710S Multi-Beam Echo Sounder (MBES) which has allowed the ship to dramatically increase the amount of data she collects in a single survey sweep. The MBES sends out a spread of sound beneath the hull, out to 65 degrees from the vertical on either side. This arc or 'swathe' moves forward as the ship does. As the echoes return the on-board computer integrates and processes them into more than 200 overlapping 'beams' of sound, each only two degrees wide. A composite picture is built up by the computer, showing the depth, profile and composition of the seabed beneath and on either side of the track.

Computer processing of the MBES returns also takes into account depth variations caused by the rise and fall of the sea and compensates for the rolling of the ship. The way sound travels through the water is affected by temperature and salinity changes so these effects are compensated for and modelled within the system.

Results can be spectacular, with detailed 3D seabed profiles being created in a single sweep. Hard material such as rock gives a strong reflection while a soft bed such as mud gives a much more muted response, all information that is useful both for navigation and for oceanographic research. The MBES picture is so detailed that it can even identify and locate shipwrecks on the seabed.

A single swathe will cover a distance to the side of up to four times the depth of water beneath the hull, a useful facility for both data collection and the safe operation of the ship. Where a survey is to be made of uncharted waters, *Endurance* can first make a scan from safer

CHAPTER FOUR - **Endurance at Work**

water, looking sideways into the unknown zone. She can them move forwards slightly then run another scan from within this 'swept' zone, looking further into the target area. In this way she can gradually move the scanned area forwards (more accurately sideways) while always remaining within an area she has checked as safe. As with all such operations, care has to be taken and the ship sailed accurately, while the scan operators need to continually monitor the progress of the scan. And if the scan is taking place in shallower waters, the swathe angle covers a narrower band of seabed, an important consideration for both data capture and the safety of the ship.

Accurate knowledge of the ship's own position is essential for the data to be of use, and on a survey, *Endurance* maps her own position to within an accuracy of a single metre. The ship uses a blend of satellite-based differential GPS combined with an inertial system with a fibre-optic laser gyro.

But, of course, it's not all high-tech. Bearings can also be taken to significant land features if they have been previously surveyed accurately. And the survey team will take visual sightings and note details of conspicuous objects that might impinge on the ability of mariners to navigate safely. They record the status of man-made items such as buoys, jetties, lights and buildings, many of which have been left by earlier whaling stations and now abandoned research stations.

Recent areas surveyed by *Endurance* include glacier 'snouts' (where then end of a glacier meets the sea and which are becoming popular destinations for cruise ships), coastal inlets and bays around South Georgia, and a complete survey around Annenkov Island, just off South Georgia.

Survey boats

Endurance's survey capability is also greatly enhanced by having two specially equipped Survey Motor Boats (SMB) on board, each equipped with echo sounding and navigation equipment. SMB *James Caird* and SMB *Nimrod* can operate inshore, in waters too restricted for *Endurance* to work, and greatly increase the rate at which *Endurance* can collect survey data.

In coastal operations, the boat crews may operate from a land-based camp for days at a time. Their first task (apart from making camp) is usually to survey and create accurately placed datum markers, from which the boats can make sure their depth measurements are carefully mapped. The crews also take tide measurements and survey data from land, although aggressive and territorial fur seals can often be a problem! A boat's paddle can be a makeshift self-defence tool, although a fast pair of legs are probably more useful. The SMBs also sometimes work with *Endurance* to provide a powerful blend of capabilities. A recent survey saw all three hulls working together to map the depths of a natural inlet known as Ardley Cove. One of the SMBs sailed slowly into the bay, taking constant depth soundings beneath its hull. *Endurance*

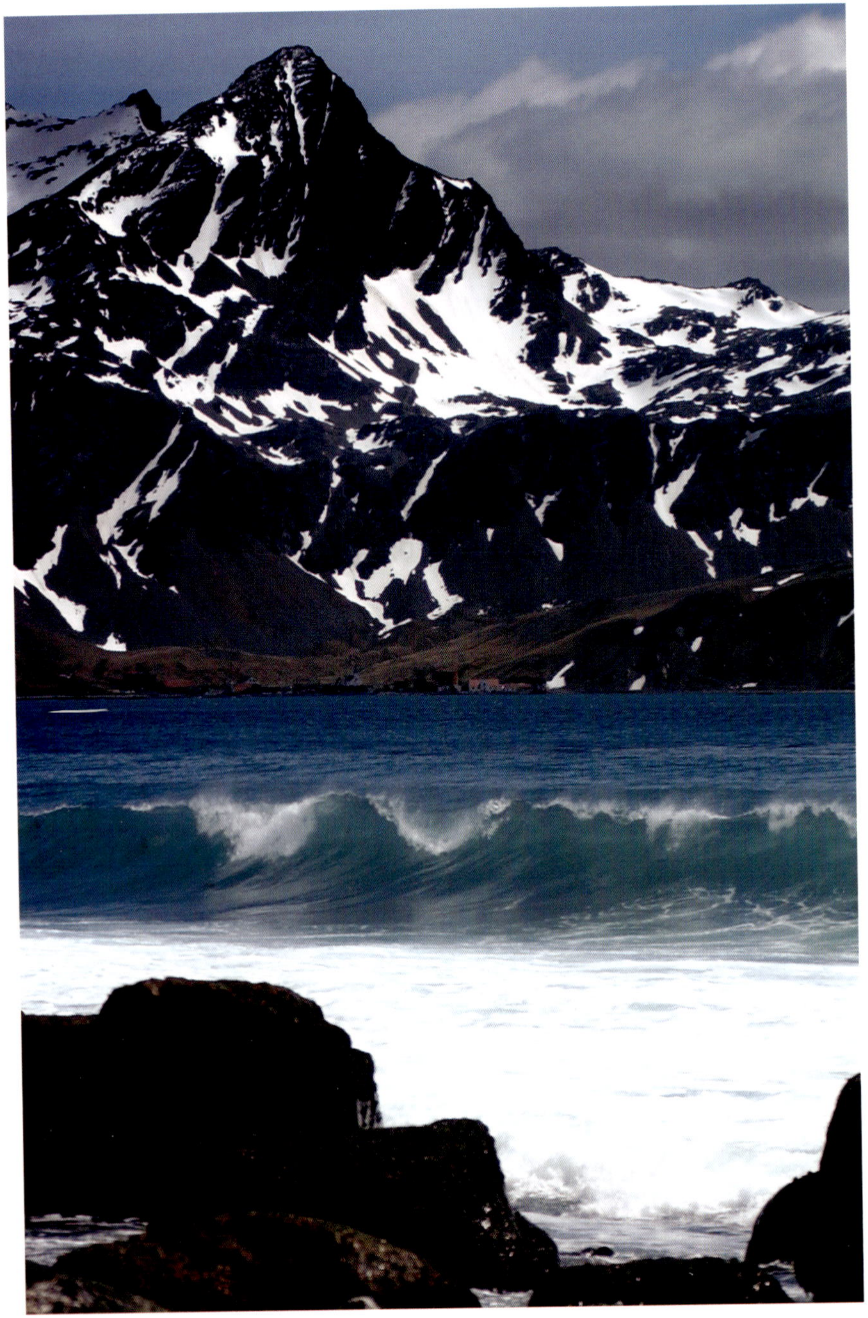

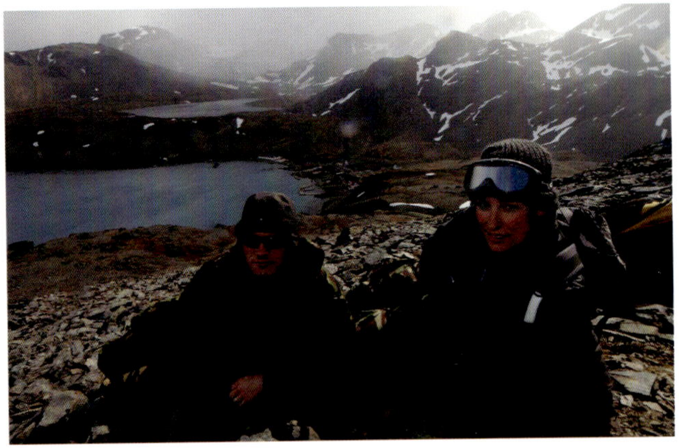

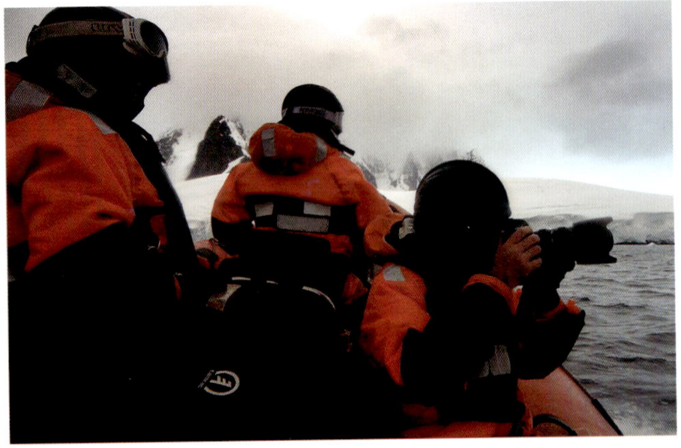

CHAPTER FOUR - **Endurance at Work**

followed slowly behind in the wake of the SMB, secure in the knowledge that in that zone at least there were no shallows or rocky outcrops hazardous to her hull. Once inside the inlet *Endurance* was able to use her MBES to survey the rest of the bay.

Oceanography

The survey department also collects and provides information on the oceans *Endurance* sails in, including those she transits through on her way to and from her operational area. Regular measurements are taken of such parameters as direction and height of waves, wind speed and direction, sea temperature, salinity and depth. More sophisticated data collection methods include the recently developed ARGO survey float. This device can be dropped over the side while en route to the Antarctic and drifts with the current, using an array of sensors to collect data. Over a 10-day cycle it sinks down to a depth of 2,000 m (6,564 ft) then returns to the surface, measuring temperature and salinity at regular intervals. The data is transmitted via satellite to the UK and is used by the Meteorological Office to help improve understanding of ocean weather systems.

Weather forecasting

Another critical role of the survey department is forecasting the weather and ice conditions to help *Endurance's* command team plan future operations. Timely warning of poor weather is especially important for the safety of helicopters and boats and allows the work packages to be replanned to create minimum disruption to the schedule. Warnings allow the ship to be secured for heavy seas, with loose items carefully tied down and the crew prepared. *Endurance* does roll heavily in bad weather, and a period of storms can impact severely on the work programme, with flying operations rendered impossible, the decks swept by heavy seas making them unsafe to cross, and with significant numbers of crew members out of action owing to seasickness. Hot food also becomes problematic as the galley becomes dangerous to cook in.

Ship's photographer

One of *Endurance's* roles is to record the state of the environment, including the ice, the wildlife, vegetation, coastlines and all the places she visits. To help with this task there is an official ship's photographer who takes images of all these. They also record the daily activities of the ship and crew, building up a library of images that help tell the story of each deployment. Other images are taken from the Lynx helicopters, while most members of the crew take their own digital cameras to capture scenes that they will remember for the rest of their lives. Most of the photographs in this book have been taken by *Endurance's* photographer and other members of the crew.

CHAPTER FOUR - **Endurance at Work**

Flight department

Endurance's helicopter flight with its two Westland Lynx Mk 3 helicopters is a powerful component of her support, survey and transport capabilities. The department is known as 212 Flight, and is an element of 815 Naval Air Squadron of the Fleet Air Arm. 815 Squadron provides all the Lynx detachments for the Fleet's warships, and is by far the largest flying squadron in the Royal Navy, although it never actually operates as a complete squadron.

The two aircraft on *Endurance* are Lynx sidenumbers 434 and 435, and are visually recognisable from other RN Lynx by the bright red panels on the doors and nose. Apart from missing some warfighting equipment they differ in little else from other Fleet Mk 3s. They are configured for landings on rough ground and snow and carry some mountings for specialist camera equipment, but their anti-icing equipment is standard. Powered by two Rolls Royce Gem gas turbine engines, the Lynx can still fly if one engine fails – a vital safety feature when flying over empty freezing seas and desolate ice-bound landscapes.

The flight has a complement of 17, including a two-person crew (Pilot and Observer) for each helicopter (usually known as 'cab' in Navy slang). The rest are divided into an Aircraft Control Petty Officer, two Senior Maintainers and two watches of five maintenance engineers. A survival gear technician rounds off the team. The engineering team individually specialise in airframes, engines, electrical and radio trades, although some of these career streams are changing and merging.

Flying from *Endurance* is extensive and demanding, with the aircrews having to face a wide range of tasks in conditions that change continually and that can become extremely dangerous very quickly. Before deploying to *Endurance*, a helicopter crew needs specialist training in mountain flying, cold weather operations, Antarctic survival and vertical photography.

Unlike most Navy helicopter operations, very few sorties are 'training' flights but are instead almost always real tasks. Crews are not normally posted here straight from training ('first tourists' in the parlance) but will have some operational experience before being posted to the ship. The normal duty period is two years, with one crew changing every year and the second-year crew acting as experienced advisors to the newcomers. One issue is that an *Endurance* helicopter crew will lose touch with their warfare skills, even though they do refresh these in simulator sessions while in the UK. But this is made up for by the variety and difficulty of flying and conditions. Pilots and Observers learn a lot here, especially in core flying and aircraft handling skills, and in dealing with very rapid changes of weather.

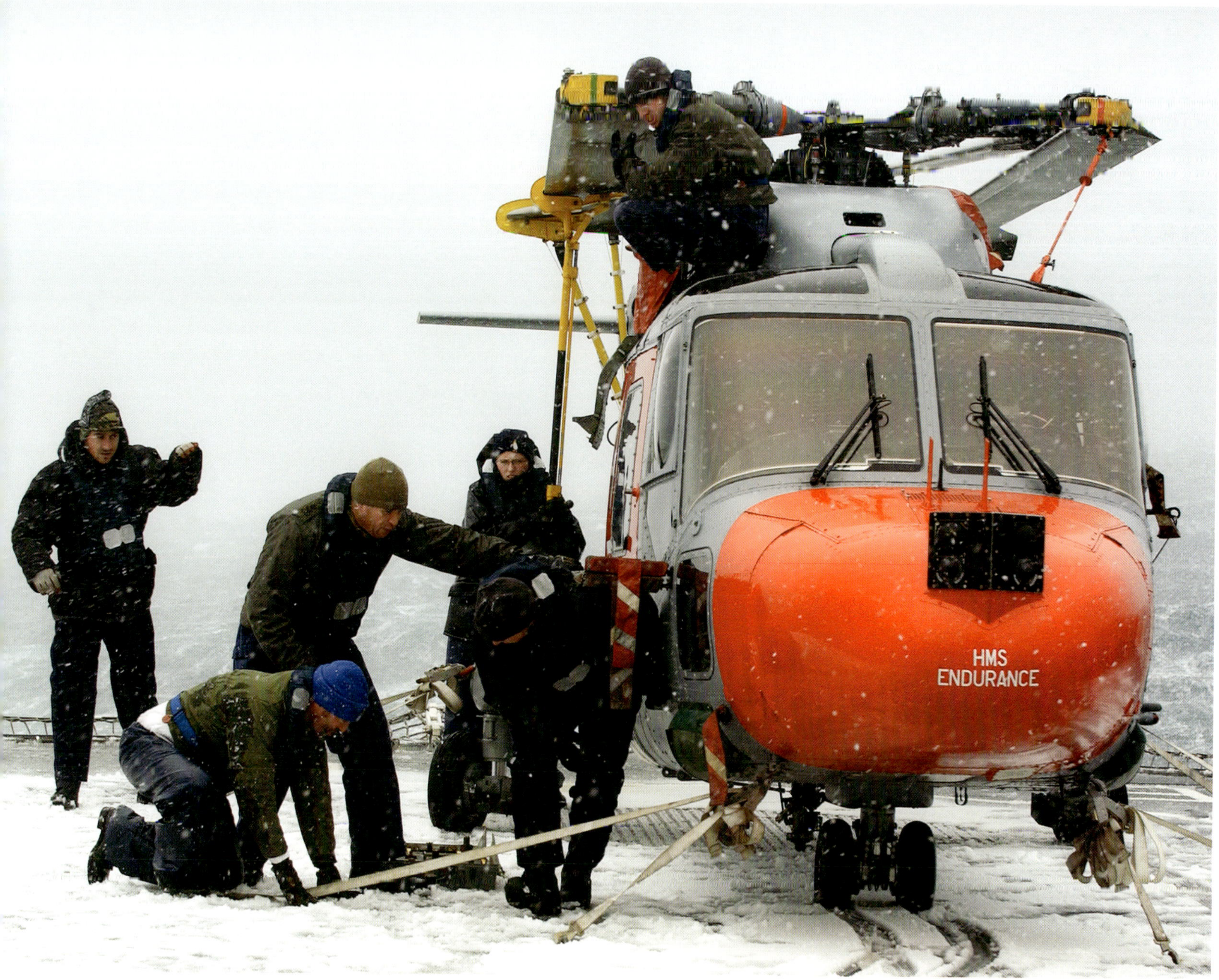
HMS
ENDURANCE

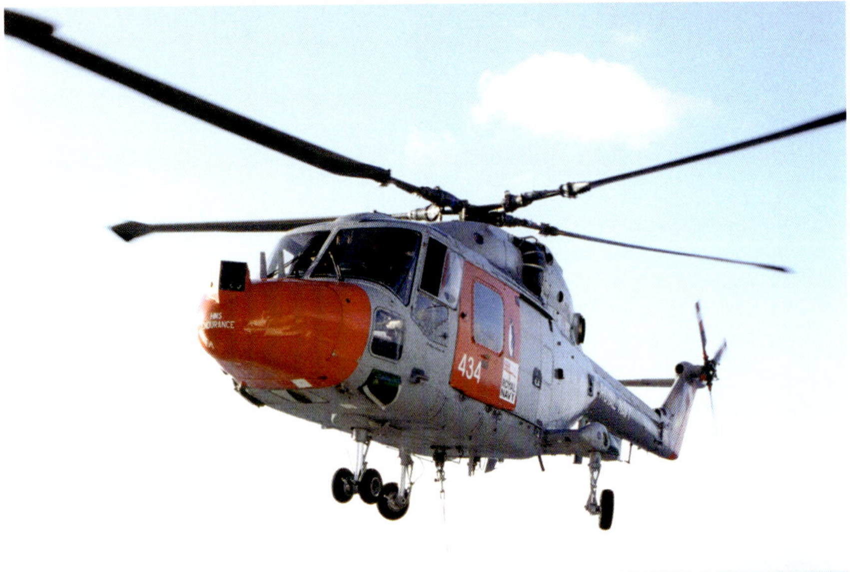
434

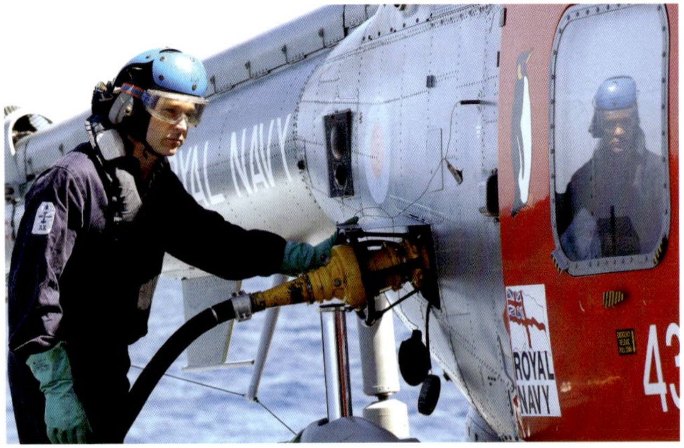
ROYAL NAVY

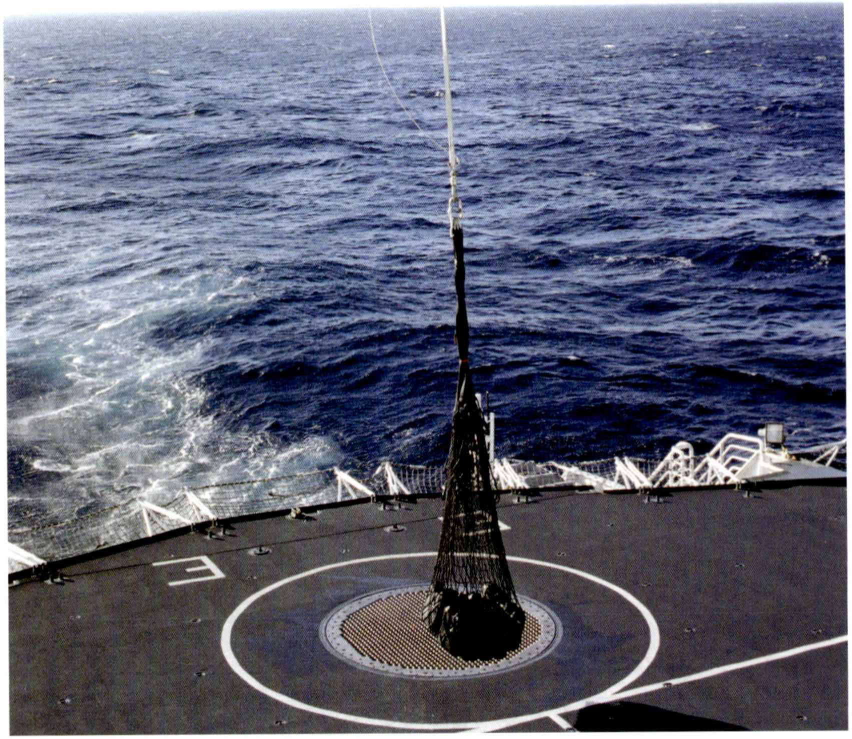

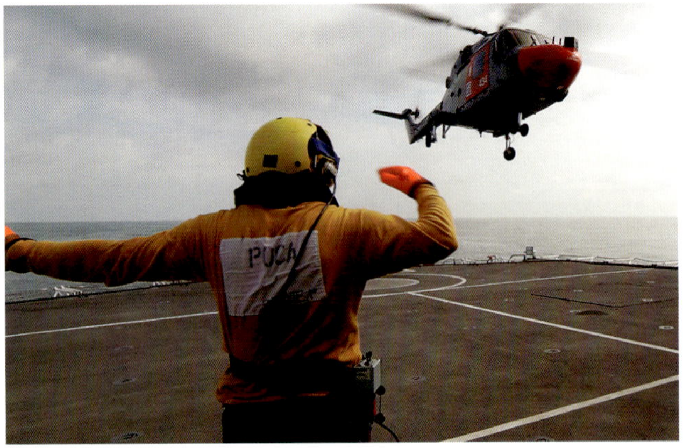

Chapter Four - Endurance at Work

As with every other role in *Endurance*, self-reliance is at a premium, and where at all possible problems have to be solved within the ship's own resources. One reason for having two helicopters is that it provides extra safety, including a self-rescue capability if one of the helicopters develops a problem. And the fact that two 'cabs' are available allows *Endurance* to generate significantly more sorties than another ship of similar size. Both airframes work hard and each crew may fly some four to six hours per day – a higher rate than almost any other RN Lynx detachment.

When the work package for any period is drawn up the planned helicopter usage is written in to it. But of course, the day-to-day work varies as weather and circumstances force the plan to change and adapt. Weather in the Antarctic has a powerful influence on flying operations, whether on the safety of personnel and aircraft, or how it affects some functions such as photography. Vertical photography tasks in particular have to wait for clear weather as they are flown at high altitudes, and opportunities have to be taken when the conditions are right, whether they are on the planned schedule or not. Some tasks may have to wait for a number of years until the availability of ship, helicopter and weather all combine.

Load carrying

A key role for the aircraft is the transport of people, equipment and materials. Antarctic terrain can be difficult and slow to travel across so air delivery is a valuable means of rapid and safe transit. Tasks can include the insertion of research scientists, the support of survey teams, and delivery of specialist equipment and transport to and from isolated communities. Scientific teams sometimes need to be ashore more than a month at a time so lots of stores need to be lifted. As well as the people, items such as tents, food, special equipment, and sometimes even transport such as quad bikes are all carried.

Large or heavy items are slung under the fuselage, often being picked up from Endurance's forward deck after they are unpacked from the hold. The load is prepared for flight by the deck team, usually being wrapped in a large cargo net. A steel or fabric strop is dropped down under the aircraft then the helicopter flown slowly into position, with the Observer hanging out the side door and giving guidance instructions to the pilot. The load is hooked on by the ground team, taking care to earth the strop first as a flying helicopter can be powerfully charged with static electricity! The Lynx then climbs away slowly and smoothly. A Lynx can carry up to 1,360 kg (3,000 lb) underneath it, about the weight of a small car. Flying with such a load can be tricky if it starts to swing, and the Pilot will have to make corrections to the flight path of the aircraft to compensate for and dampen any load movement. If the cargo movement gets too much it can be jettisoned, but careful loading and flying should prevent any problems getting to this stage. Very light loads will swing about easily so weights are sometimes added for stability.

CHAPTER FOUR - **Endurance at Work**

Landing in the Arctic can be challenging, especially if delivering people and equipment high up a mountain, where the thinner air affects aircraft performance. And white snow or ice often doesn't have enough visual cues for holding a hovering helicopter so sometimes a coloured smoke grenade is dropped to give both an aiming mark and indication of wind speed and direction.

Survey photography

Another task for the flying team is survey photography, whether vertical or oblique. For oblique photography the Observer leans out of the door with the camera while the helicopter transits at about 300–600 m (1,000–2,000 ft).

Vertical photography is more technically elaborate and is used for surveys, mapping and to record changes to the environment and coastline. In this case a specialist camera is attached to the side of the aircraft in a large red fairing. The helicopter is flown very accurately on a planned track at around 2,400 m (8,000 ft), with the Observer using a periscope through the cabin floor to aim the camera. Vertical photography can only be carried out in clear weather, so is often scheduled out as an opportunity task. Flying at this height in a draughty helicopter is cold enough in temperate climates – but in the Antarctic, temperatures here can be as low as minus 19 degrees C. Aircrew will wear between five to nine separate layers of clothing, including three pairs of gloves!

Such mapping and scientific work are not the only photography tasks that the Lynx can be asked to do. HMS *Endurance* often transports and supports crews for film and television documentaries, and recent missions including flying with a specially modified BBC camera mounted outside for a major wildlife documentary series.

Logistics department

The work of the Logistics Department is probably more varied than that of any other department, from the management of stores and supplies, the organisation of resupply and crew movements, general administration and pay, catering, to the provision of medical services. Every day sees a different set of problems to be solved. And as with every other department, logistics personnel have important secondary roles, such as providing the Damage Control Officer, the Standing Sea Emergency Party and members of firefighting teams.

CHAPTER FOUR - Endurance at Work

Supply

Extensive planning begins in the six months before deployment, where the logistics team decide on the necessary stores of consumables and spares, basing their decisions on historical data, known reliability figures and prior experience. In particular, the Lynx helicopters need extensive stocks of spares, although accurate fleet-wide reliability figures help in deciding what's needed. Stores and spares are ordered about 12 weeks before *Endurance* sets sail. And when at sea, the ship's Stores Accountants manage the myriad of different items that are taken on board; some 3,000 stock lines valued at over £1.5 million.

The stores team are also responsible for organising the delivery of items such as spare parts when at sea. Stores can be flown from the UK (or Norway!) by commercial airline to the next port of call, usually in South America, and delivered by contract agent. Other options include delivery by commercial charter or military aircraft to the Falkland Islands. Important spares and supplies can be dropped into the sea by parachute from an RAF C130 Hercules transport flying from the Falklands. The load has to be well packed and watertight so that it floats for long enough for the Endurance to recover it!

The British Antarctic Survey has also helped by using their aircraft or allowing their bases to be used as collection points. And in the lonely spaces of the Antarctic, bases and research teams from all countries cooperate and help each other, allowing the use of their aircraft or airstrips.

Catering

The catering team deliver three meals a day, seven days a week. And when the ship moves to 24-hour operations so do they, providing extra meals when required. A Petty Officer Caterer manages a close-knit team that includes four Leading Chefs, four Chefs and Stewards. The catering department is responsible for provisioning the ship while keeping to tight budgetary constraints, and just before *Endurance* deploys, food for 180 days is loaded into her freezers and storerooms.

Different ranks usually eat in their respective messes, although the standard of cooking is equally high in all of them. The caterers work hard to keep the food interesting, with menus ranging from traditional English breakfasts to vegetarian cutlets, from roast lamb to chicken korma. They also manage to meet the special needs of some crew members who need individual diets for health, religious or ethical reasons. Providing a varied and interesting menu over a long deployment is a challenge, and the team always take the opportunity to top up with fresh food during visits to overseas ports.

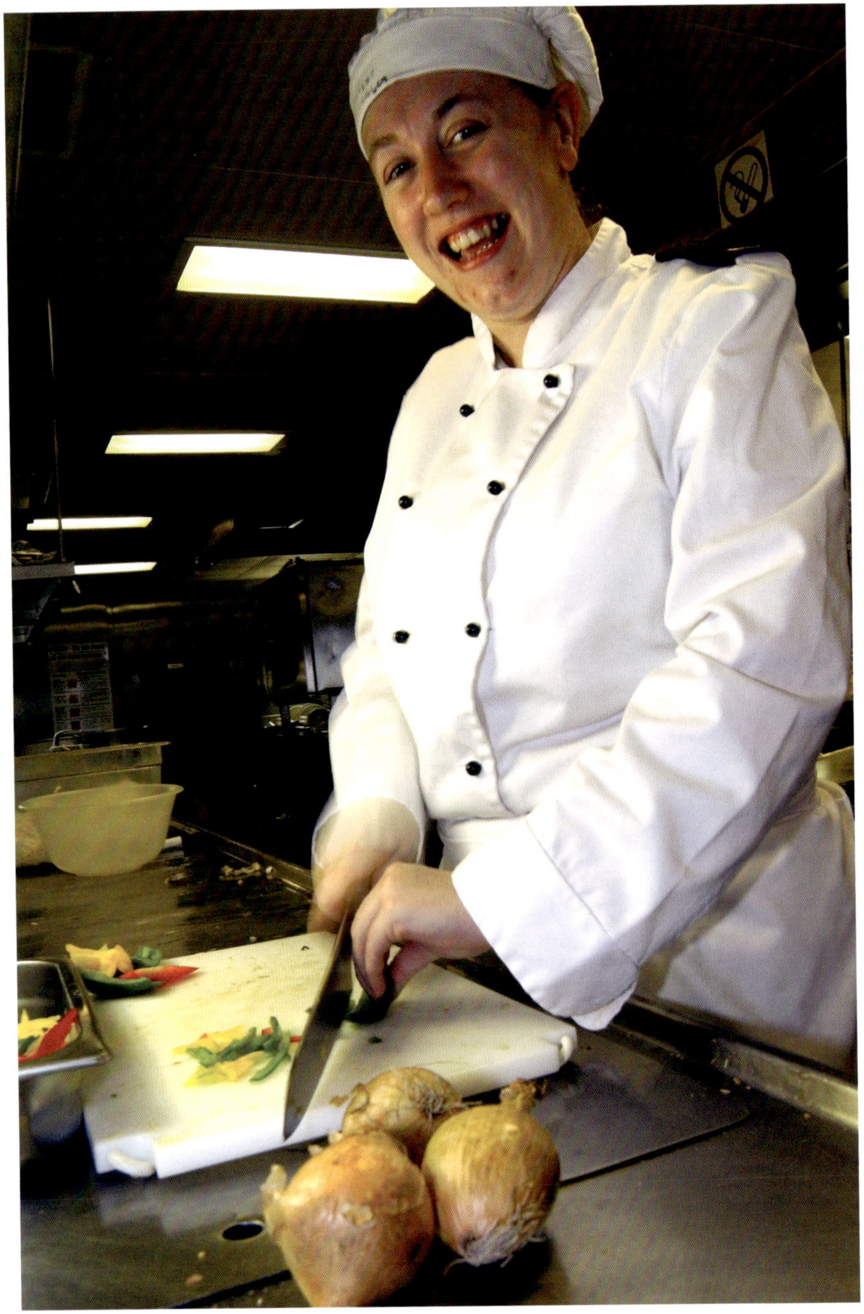

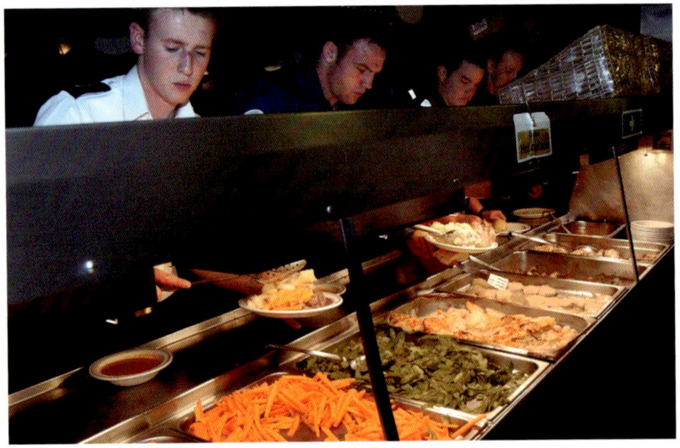

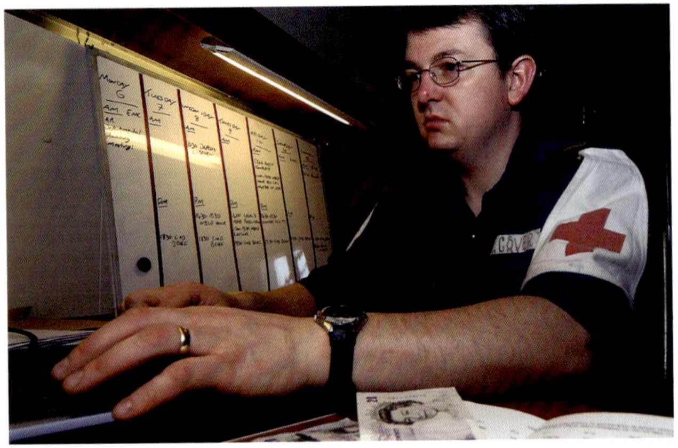

CHAPTER FOUR - **Endurance at Work**

When carrying out her defence diplomacy role, *Endurance* often entertains local dignitaries during port visits. On these occasions the Chefs and Stewards are able to demonstrate their hospitality and cooking skills to a wider audience, and enjoy 'putting on a show'. Such specialist hospitality can also be extended to senior visitors at home, and the catering team were honoured to serve Her Majesty the Queen when HMS *Endurance* became the Royal host ship during the Trafalgar 200 commemorations.

Administration

The logistics department manages the general administration of the ship and her crew. In the Royal Navy, administration and accounting staff are known by their traditional title of 'Writers'. In civilian terms they may be thought of as HR specialists, although their remit is much wider than that. They provide advice and guidance on personnel issues, travel, leave, general promotion, discipline and naval law. One of their more popular roles is sorting out foreign currency for crewmembers going ashore in overseas ports. And as crew members leave or join the ship during deployment they organise travel and pay arrangements.

NAAFI

As with almost any British service establishment there is a NAAFI shop on board. NAAFI (Naval, Army and Air Force Institutes) is the trading arm of the Ministry of Defence, and for may years has provided canteens, shops and other facilities to British servicemen and women around the world. On *Endurance*, the small shop sells food items, confectionery, cigarettes and other small comfort items. It is staffed by civilians, although they are civilians who wear uniform and who play a full part in the running of the ship and its various emergency teams.

Medical department

The role of the medical department is to maintain the effectiveness of the ship and her company. To do this they have more equipment and stores than a normal RN ship of this size, as *Endurance* regularly operates at great distances from any support or land-based medical facilities. The ship has both a sick bay and a second medical ward, while an on-board Oxygen Concentrator allows oxygen to be produced from atmospheric air without the need to store large high-pressure cylinders.

The Royal Navy has a wealth of experience and knowledge from operating in all areas of the world, all available to the medical team when planning for deployment. From this information the Doctor provides advice to the Command team on the risks and impact of infectious illness. *Endurance* is a small enclosed community, so in theory an infectious disease could spread very rapidly and have a significant impact on the ship's operations. But as the ship operates far from large population bases, and her crew is fit, healthy, well-screened, and thoroughly immunised, such problems are rare. The medical teams still have to deal with a range of conditions though, such as colds, coughs, basic dental problems, the occasional trauma injury and particular problems caused by the extreme cold. And, of course, when the ship is rolling and pitching in a storm, there is a steady demand for treatments to help deal with seasickness.

Should there be a major incident the on-board team has a basic surgical capability, albeit using battlefield anaesthetic. But in almost all cases the preferred option is to stabilise a casualty then evacuate to a hospital environment. Helicopters can transport a patient and care team either to the final destination or to an airfield from where a fixed wing air ambulance can take over.

And medical care is one area where international cooperation in the Antarctic can be seen in action. Close ties with the British Antarctic Survey mean that their medical and transport resources can be used if necessary, while medical teams from both organisations meet pre-deployment to exchange information and carry out medical teaching. If necessary *Endurance* would offer transport and medical facilities to BAS or other groups, whatever the nationality, and most of them would do likewise. The Antarctic is a lonely, dangerous place, and those that live and work there will help each other out, especially in an emergency.

Chaplain

Endurance may sail with a Chaplain on board who, like all forces chaplains, works in an interfaith, interdenominational setting. Whether a crew member is of a Christian denomination, follows another religion or has none, the Chaplain's role is to provide spiritual, moral and pastoral support as well as being a friend and advisor to all onboard.

Any individual Chaplain can only fully meet the spiritual needs of those from his or her own religious and denominational group, but the Chaplain will always take care when giving pastoral or moral advice so as to respect the teachings of the faith of the person seeking help. He or she can also call on support from other service and civilian chaplains who come from other faith groups.

The Chaplain can only conduct those services as authorised to do by their own church, although every attempt is made to include as many of the ships company as possible, where the teaching of their own faith allows. Should a person from a non-Christian faith join the crew, the

CHAPTER FOUR - **Endurance at Work**

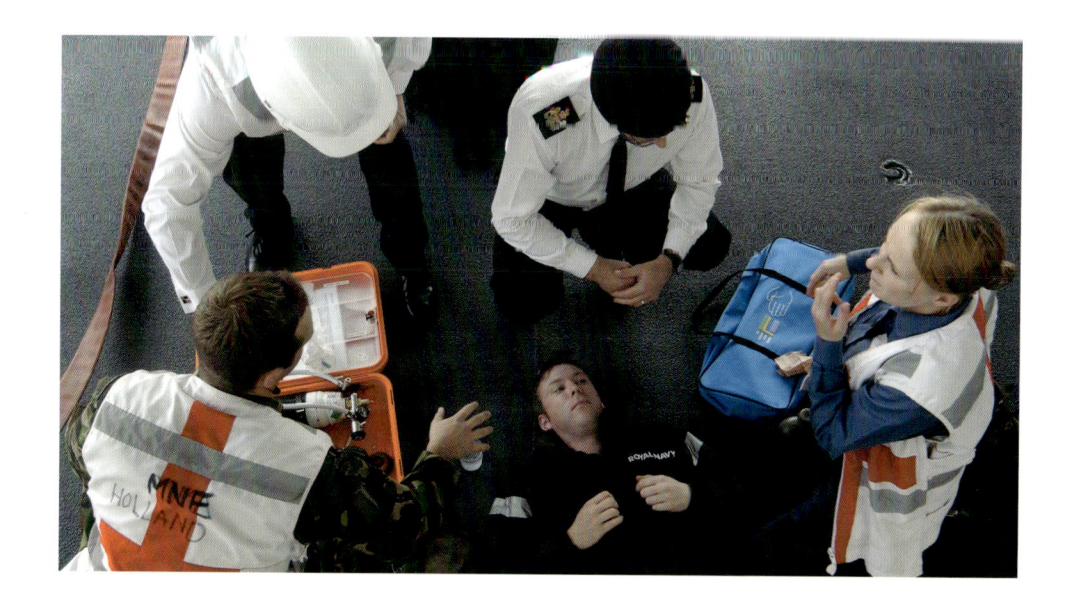

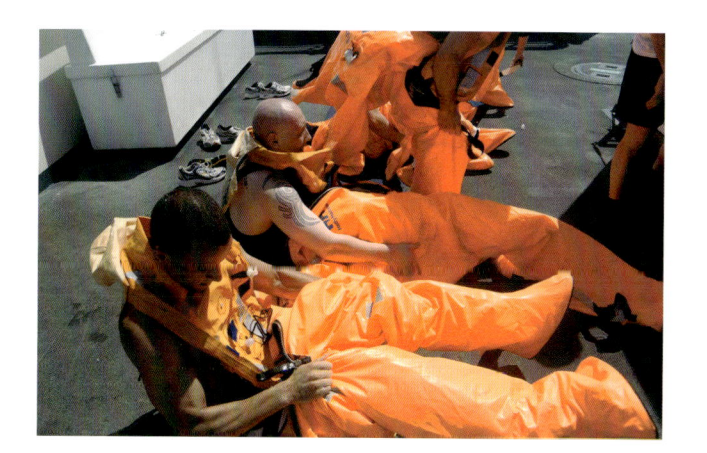

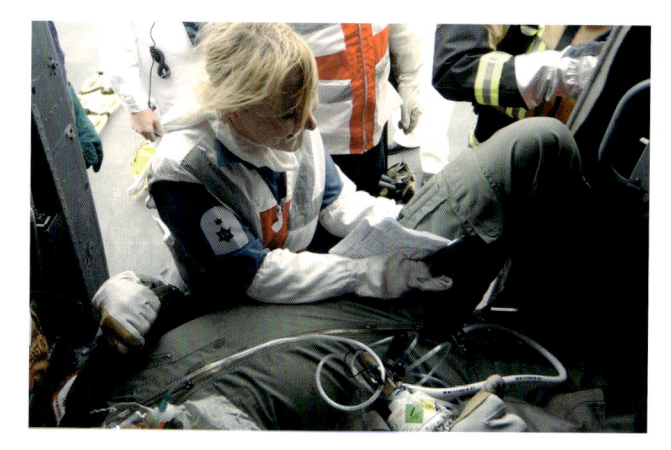

THE RED PLUM   71   **HMS Endurance**

Chaplin will give all the support they can to allow that crewmember to worship in accordance with their own religion.

Apart from the formal religious role, it is essential that the Chaplain keeps him or herself accessible to all crew members. They can often be the first point of contact when a crew member has personal problems, perhaps faced on-board, perhaps from events taking place back home. Often the job is merely taking time to listen and chat, but in other cases the Chaplain can provide advice, or even instigate support actions such as compassionate leave or support from the Navy Families Service back home.

Much of the Chaplain's day is spent working around the ship, 'loitering with intent' and chatting to people. It often means helping with the daily work of the ship, whether in the galley, the engine spaces, the bridge or elsewhere. And when things are going well it can appear that there isn't much to do. Which is a good sign. If the Chaplain is very busy it is normally because of a serious problem such as death or serious accident, whether onboard or at home. Not a happy time perhaps, but one where the true value of the Chaplain can be seen.

Keeping safe

The sea can be an unpredictable and dangerous place, and the daily operations of ship and aircraft pose their own hazards. Where *Endurance* goes, she is unlikely to be able to call for help that will arrive quickly. So it's up to the crew to look after themselves and their ship. Everyone, irrespective of their rank, has to undertake basic firefighting and emergency training. And should a problem arise, everyone, no matter their department, rank or appointment, has a role to play.

NBCD (Nuclear, Biological and Chemical Defence) is the Navy term for such operations, although in *Endurance's* case the risks are mainly non-combat, such as possible fires, collisions and other accidents. The ship has a small group of qualified NBCD ratings led by the Chief Stoker who have undergone rigorous training at HMS *Excellent*, a land-based school renowned for the thoroughness, toughness and realism of its training. NBCD-qualified ratings will have been put through the wringer in numerous exercises, including trying to 'save' a simulated ship, complete with flooding compartments, fuel and oil fires and simulated casualties.

The NBCD team form the core of the Standing Sea Emergency Party and also have a responsibility to provide training to the whole Ship's Company. This can range from simple refresher presentations to practical problem-solving and large-scale exercises. Such training also forms a considerable part of pre-deployment preparation, where the crew is still learning to work as an effective team.

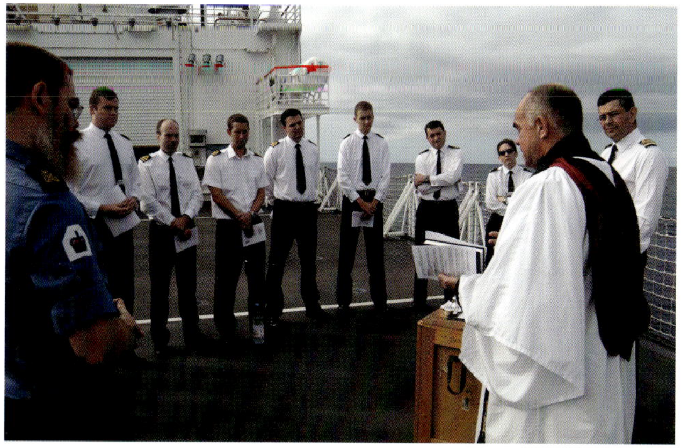

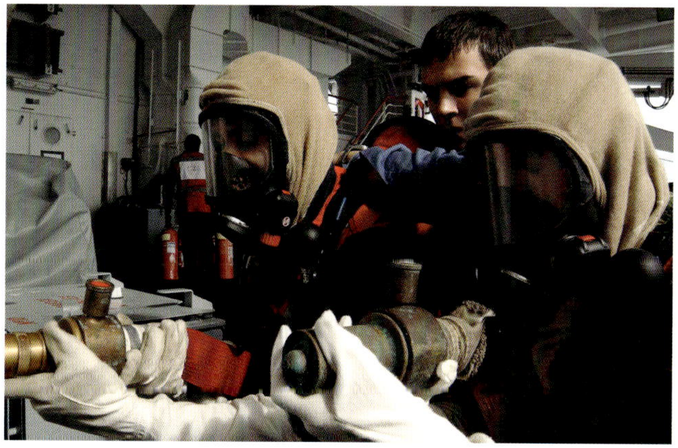

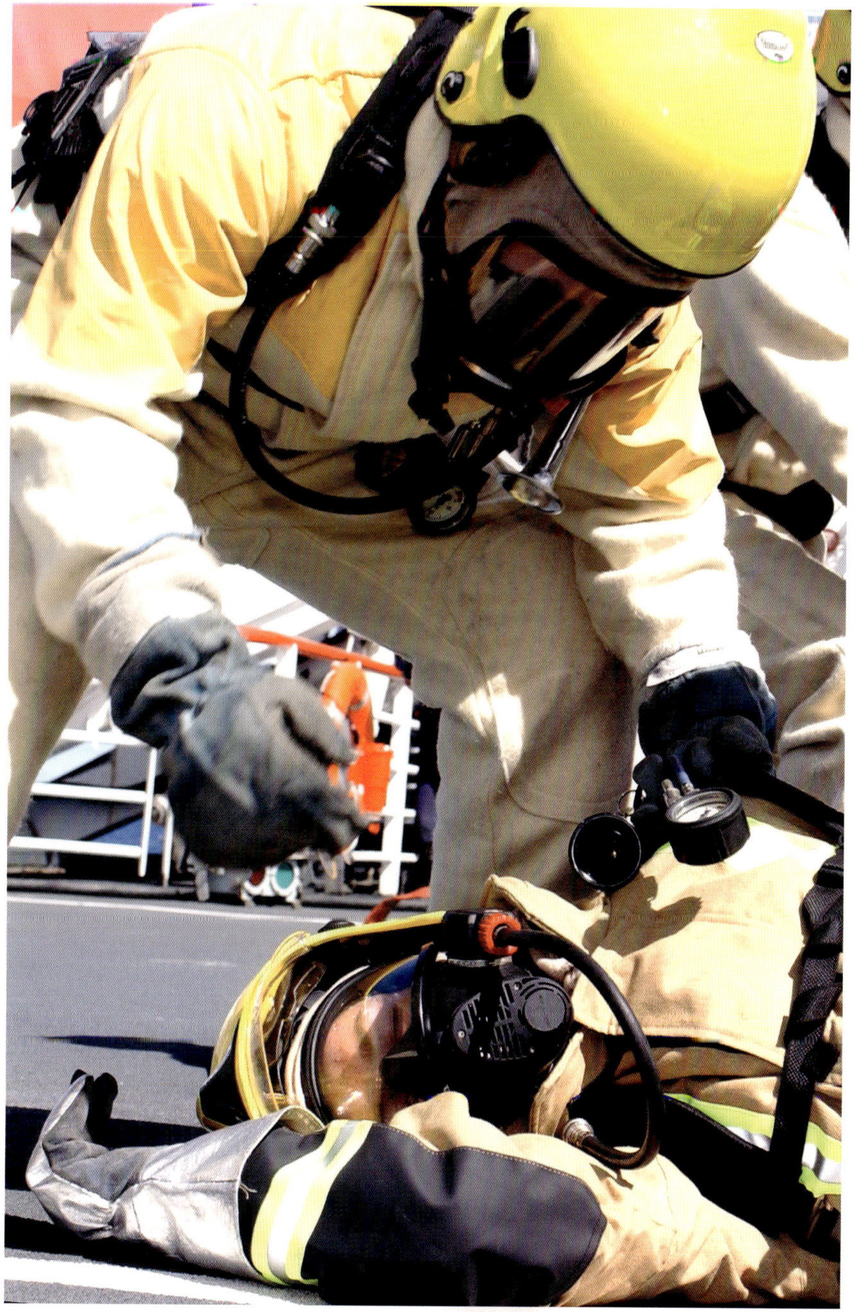

CHAPTER FOUR - **Endurance at Work**

Testing times

Before *Endurance* (or any other RN ship) deploys she has a period of work-up and Operational Service Training (OST), with every department working hard to get their equipment, procedures and skills up to standard. This period climaxes in a Final Inspection, where an external team puts the ship and crew through a series of practice situations. Assessors spring various emergency scenarios, including man overboard drills, power failures, system failures, fires, explosions, flooding and collision. The scenarios can change as the simulated situation develops, with the assessors suddenly 'disabling' ship's systems or blocking passageways to see how effectively the crew adapts.

Endurance's history and Norwegian civilian construction poses unusual problems for both assessors and crew, as many of her systems and procedures are different from the Fleet standard, and some scenarios don't apply. It's a hard workup, but by the end of it *Endurance* and her crew are ready to face the worst that the sea and weather can throw at them, secure in their ability to cope with the unexpected and able to rely on their own expertise and initiative.

Defence diplomacy

An important role for *Endurance* is defence diplomacy. This expression covers events such as visits to foreign ports, hosting receptions and dinners for dignitaries and meeting with local people of all kinds. It all helps to promote the UK's image and interests around the world and to build personal contacts with foreign governments, navies and civilians. And as *Endurance's* role is so closely identified with conservation and preservation of the environment she normally gets a warm welcome wherever she goes.

Diplomacy often works best at the personal level, where every member of *Endurance's* becomes an ambassador for Britain. A recent example is when the Chaplain instigated contacts with a local religious community run by four nuns, who provide a home for physically and mentally disabled males between the ages of 6 and 88 in Puerto Belgrano, Argentina. The Ship's Company volunteered to redecorate and generally spruce up the school buildings. Another example was when during *Endurance's* recent visit to Ushuaia, Argentina, a joint laying of wreaths ceremony was held at the invitation of Argentine veterans to commemorate the fallen of both sides in the 1982 South Atlantic conflict.

Chapter Four - Endurance at Work

Aid

Such diplomacy can also move into more practical help. A disciplined well-trained crew who come complete with medical support, communications equipment, transport aircraft and lots of practical skills can be a vital asset when natural disaster strikes or when people need help to overcome environmental or other emergencies.

It's not all work

The crew work hard, especially when the various work packages are in progress, but they do have spare time which they can fill in a number of ways.

Movies are played in the mess, although many people now have their own portable TVs, DVD players, iPods and the like. And with 230v electricity supplied to the cabin and living spaces they don't need to bring six months' supply of batteries with them either. The ship even has one cabin that can be used as a library or study room, complete with a collection of books donated by friends, family and supporters. This space is quite important, as many crew members need time and space to study, whether for promotion or for general educational qualifications.

Most share only two or three to a cabin, so it's a little easier to find some privacy, peace and quiet than on a warship. The cabins themselves are more comfortable, more like a passenger ferry than a warship. Most have en-suite sink, shower and toilets (heads).

Keeping physically fit in the confines of a ship can be a challenge, especially where a team of skilled chefs produce three solid meals a day! So a small gym has been created and is popular with off-duty crew members, helped by the PTI. On recent deployments the Ship's Company has set up a 'Polar Challenge', where people run, row, step or cycle in their regular gym sessions, with their combined 'distance' added together. The target distance for the ship was 20,250 km (12,273 miles), the distance from the North to the South Pole. To achieve this the crew had to complete an average of 107 km (65 miles) for every day at sea.

Chapter Four - Endurance at Work

Other sporting competitions include inter-departmental triathlons, 'runathons' and the Captain's Deployment Cup. Displaying perhaps more enthusiasm than skill, teams from different departments compete for this in contests such as volleyball, tug-of-war, rowing and cricket and, of course, cake-decorating...

The crew take all the opportunities they are given to get ashore, whether the ship is in a foreign harbour or out in the wildness of the South Atlantic. One of the reasons many join the Navy is to see something of the world, and those serving on Endurance get to see places no other RN vessel does. If weather, schedule and safety permits, some are able to take part in more adventurous journeys, including self-organised climbing expeditions and even canoe trips around the icy coastlines.

Other special events are organised, usually before or after the work packages begin, often when *Endurance* is in transit between the UK and the South Atlantic. These can have a training objective as well as a fun one. For example, *Endurance* regularly runs an 'It's a Knockout' competition, where teams move around different stands to carry out competitive tasks for which they get points. All the task are related to Nuclear, Biological and Chemical Defence (NBCD) training and include exercises in damage control, firefighting, first-aid, survival, casualty evacuation etc. While light-hearted, the competition does involve the demonstration of correct techniques, the correct use of equipment and the need for teamwork and leadership.

And have you ever heard of a village fete at sea? *Endurance* holds one, with each department organising different stalls and events, mainly on the quarterdeck and hangar deck. Competitions such as who can grow the best (and worst) beard are also popular. And of course, like any village fete, the weather can change rapidly and rain on the festivities. But at least the *Endurance* 'Fete Committee' have some of the best weather forecasters in the business working for them.

Mariners of all nations traditionally make a big event of 'crossing the line', when their ship crosses the equator from one hemisphere to the other. On the day the line is crossed, the 'Court of King Neptune' summons newly joined members of the crew on deck to be tried for various misdemeanours, real or imaginary. Defendants are invariably found guilty and their sentence involves some form of light-hearted punishment and a soaking in the specially constructed swimming pool. Miscreants are usually younger crew members who have never 'crossed the line' before, but senior ratings and officers are not immune. Wiser heads make sure they are wearing old clothes before they appear in front of the King and Queen of the Deep.

Chapter Four - Endurance at Work

CHAPTER FIVE

Where she goes

Every year, *Endurance* sets off on her long journey south, leaving Portsmouth for a trip that will last for at least half the year. Her normal deployment places her in Antarctic waters during the southern summer (from October to May) so that she doesn't have to face the worst of the winter weather and ice.

The first part of the deployment is the transit south, through the tropics and across the equator into the South Atlantic and eventually the Southern Ocean. During this period the crew make final preparations for her work packages, carry out various training exercises and bring the new joiners up to speed. *Endurance* will also 'show the flag' with port visits to such countries as Portugal, Brazil, Uruguay, Argentina and others. Such visits are also an opportunity for the crew to go ashore and see something of a foreign country and people one of the reasons why many of them joined the Navy in the first place. The ship will often make similar stops on the journey back at the end of the deployment.

Her main operational area is the Antarctic region, which begins at 60 degrees south. But she also works above that line, around the sub-Antarctic islands such as the Falklands, South Georgia and the South Sandwich Islands.

The Falkland Islands

The Falklands are one of the largest island groups in the South Atlantic and lie about 480 km (300 miles) east of the South American coast. Some 200 islands form the group, and the two large main islands are home to a resident population of about 2,400 people plus a few hundred stationed military personnel. Most of them live in and around Stanley on East Falkland, the capital and largest city.

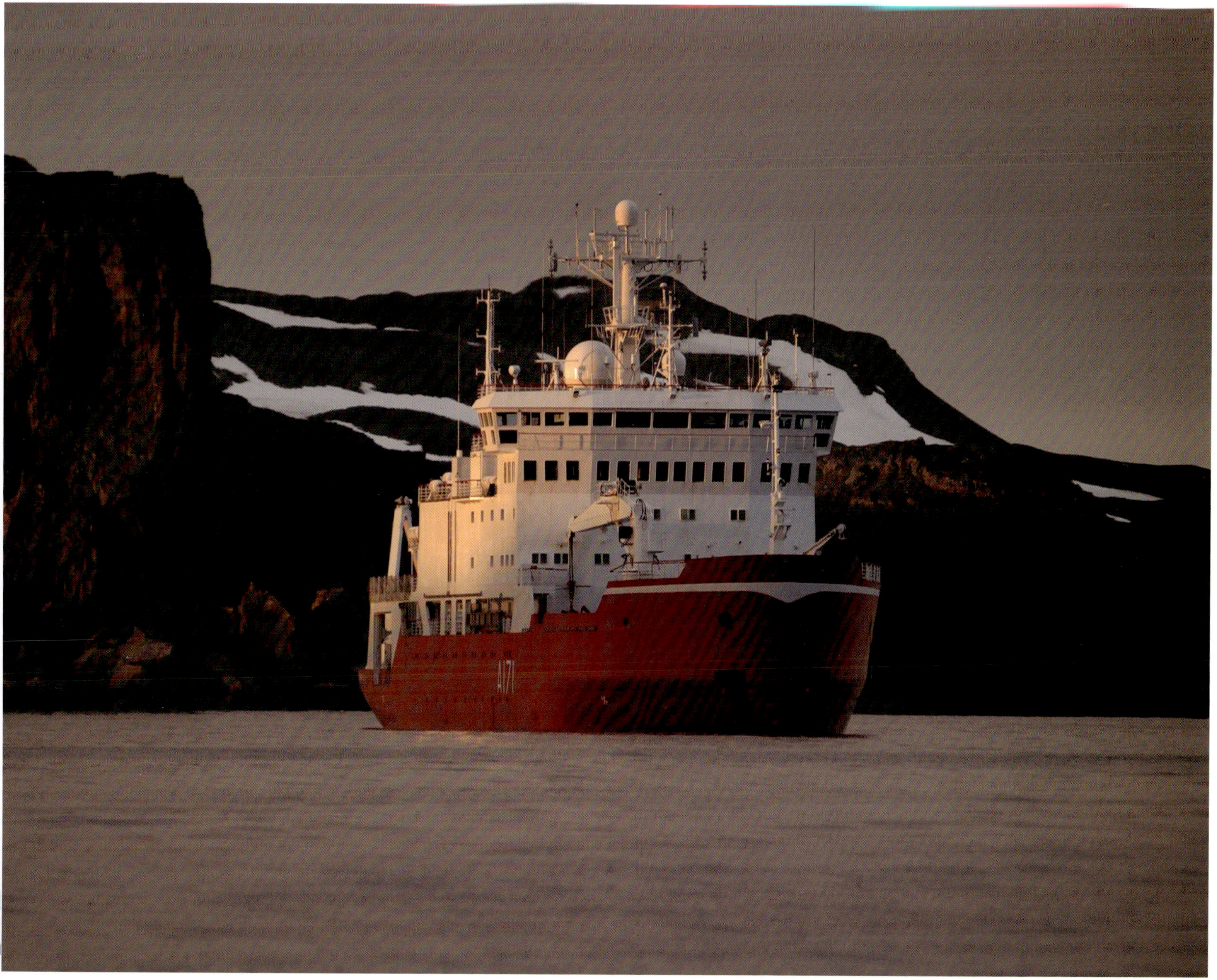
A171

CHAPTER FIVE - **Where She Goes**

Elephant Seals on the beach at King Edwards Point, South Georgia seem unperturbed by their new neighbour

South Atlantic Fur Seals are now a common sight on the beaches of South Georgia

The King Penguin lives up to its regal name.   All Photographs © Tony Hall

Chapter Five - Where She Goes

A self-governing Overseas Territory of the UK, the Falklands are also the subject of long-standing claims to sovereignty by Argentina. After the 1982 conflict with Argentina, Britain now maintains a sizeable military commitment on the island and a warship on patrol in the surrounding seas. A by-product of this presence is the airport at Mount Pleasant, which has opened up the island to transport flights direct from the UK and chartered airline flights from Chile.

The terrain varies from boggy moorland to rugged mountains and coastal inlets, and is largely empty apart from a few scattered settlements and farms. Much of the terrain is treeless and relatively bare, covered in tussocky grass, scree and small boulders. This unspoilt and almost uninhabited landscape allows wildlife such as birds, seabirds, penguins and seals to thrive. The islands also have the world's biggest colony of rockhopper penguins.

Endurance regularly visits, both to 'show the flag', and to use the harbour facilities to refuel and resupply. International air links mean that personnel who need to return to the UK can leave the ship here to fly back. And crew members scheduled to join the ship during deployment will usually route via the Falklands.

The islanders themselves have traditionally survived on sheep farming and in earlier times the farming of seaweed (kelp). But in recent years the income from fishing and tourism has become mainstays of the economy. Exploratory drilling has also shown that significant oil deposits may exist in the surrounding waters. So the challenge facing the Falklands government is to manage the exploitation of these and the fish stocks in such a way that the environment is left damaged and the way of life preserved.

South Georgia

Much further south is the island of South Georgia. Long, narrow, mountainous and rugged, South Georgia has been described as "breathtakingly beautiful and a sight on an early spring day not easily forgotten". Most of the island consists of two mountain ranges, of which 11 peaks reach up to over 2000 m (6550 ft). The rocky high ground is interspersed with deep valleys, many holding large glaciers that lead to the sea. Much of the island is covered in snow and ice, with the higher ground covered all year round. But the coastal regions support a spectacular array of seabirds, penguins and mammals such as seals. Whales also regularly appear in the surrounding waters.

South Georgia (together with the South Sandwich Islands further to the southeast) has the status of a UK Overseas Territory. The island is isolated, being over 2,100 km (1,300 miles) from South America and nearly 1400 km (870 miles) from the Falkland Islands. But it is as close to the South Pole as northern England is to the North Pole.

There is no native population there, although the British Atlantic Survey maintains two research stations. Two museum curators and a marine officer and his wife complete the permanent population. This is supplemented by visitors from licensed fishing vessels, tourist ships, conservation groups, fishery protection ships and other visitors, including, of course, HMS *Endurance*.

The island is a popular destination for tourists, who come to appreciate the wild landscape and vibrant wildlife. The abandoned whaling station at Grytviken is also a much-visited destination and the manager's villa there has been developed into a museum of whaling and South Georgia life.

As with other Antarctic locations, allowing fishing and tourism to take place without destroying the very environment that attracts them is a careful and difficult balancing act. The large population of albatrosses is especially vulnerable to being caught in fishing gear and a conservation campaign is promoting measures to protect them while allow fishing to continue.

Endurance regularly visits South Georgia and its surrounding outlying islands, partly in her role as patrol ship, and partly to build up an accurate survey of the surrounding waters. By mapping the seabed with her sounding systems she can enable other ships, especially tour ships, to operate safely around the rocky and desolate coastlines.

South Shetlands

Further south again, the South Shetland Islands sit below the 60 degrees parallel and are regarded as true Antarctic islands. They are only some 120 km (75 miles) from the tip of the Antarctic peninsula. The islands are designated as a Specially Managed Area and are protected under an agreement by Argentina, Spain, Norway, Chile, the UK and the USA.

Deception Island is one of this group, and has become a much-visited destination by scientists and tourist cruises. The island has a narrow horseshoe shape with a protected natural harbour inside the horseshoe and entered through a narrow channel with steep, high rocky 'walls'. Deception is actually the top of a volcano and this central harbour is the 'caldera' or crater. It is one of the few places in the world where a ship can sail right into the centre of an active volcano.

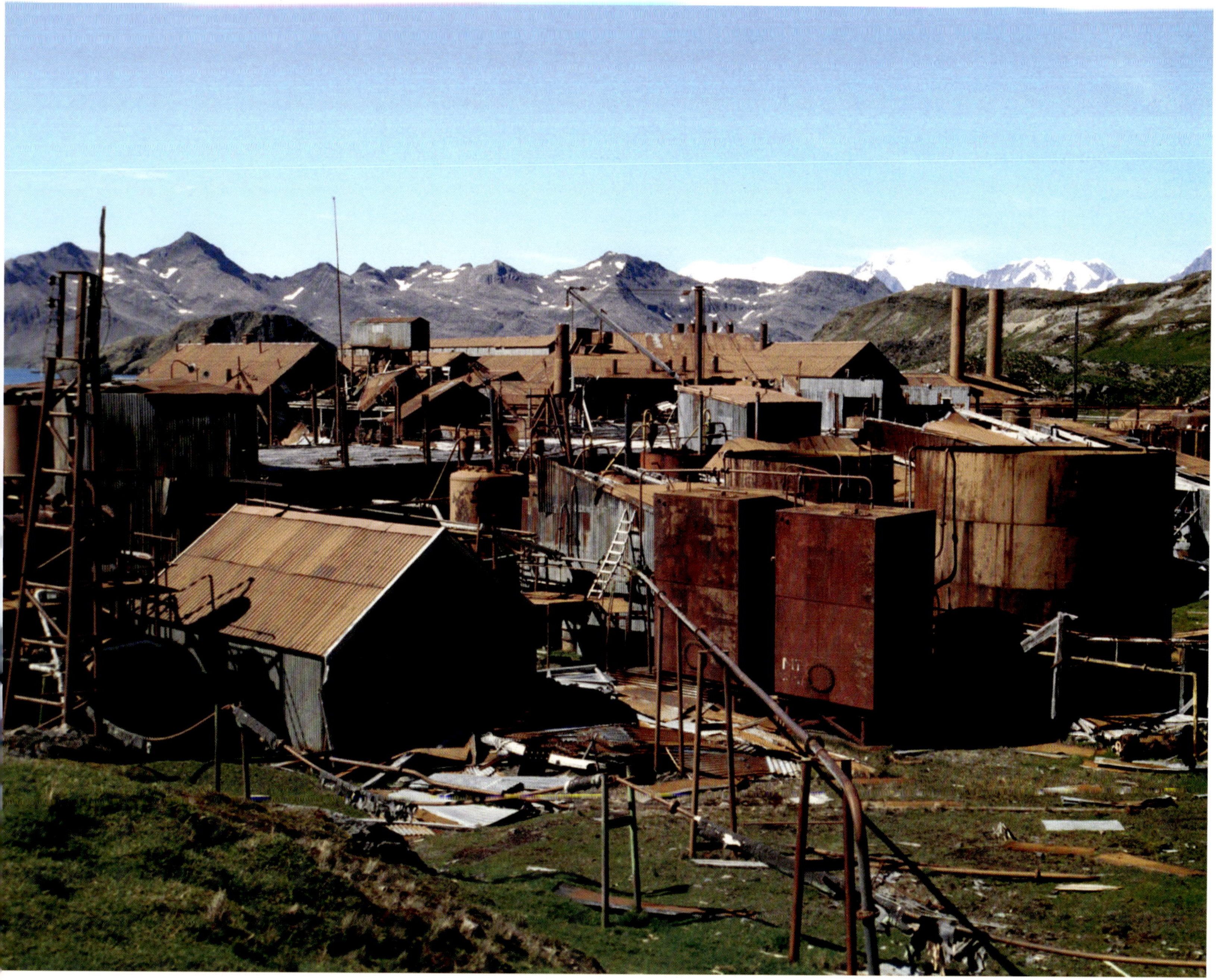

Chapter Five - Where She Goes

Like other islands this far south, Deception has been host in the past to whalers and seal-hunters. They are gone now, and the only residents are the scientists at the Spanish and Argentinean research stations manned during the Antarctic summer months. *Endurance* has regular contact with the residents of both bases and has carried out hydrographic surveys around the island and surrounding waters.

Over 150,000 seabirds make their home here, while other wildlife live on the ice-free slopes. Tourists come here regularly, amazed by the rugged scenery and abundant bird and mammal life. Volcanic geothermic activity creates plenty of hot springs and vents so visitors can bathe in naturally hot water – not bad for below the Antarctic Circle!

But the volcano can still be dangerous. It has a history of regular eruptions, and the remains of abandoned whaling stations, fisheries and research stations stand testament to the risks of staying here. The last major eruption was only in 1970, so today's scientists make sure they monitor the volcano's behaviour closely and have emergency procedures in place should they have to leave in a hurry.

King George Island is largest of the South Shetland Islands, and has more research activities taking place there than anywhere else in Antarctica. Nine permanent stations belong to Argentina, Brazil, Chile, China, South Korea, Peru, Poland, Russia, and Uruguay. Chile maintains the only airstrip while the Russian station has the most southern Orthodox Church in the world, complete with priest.

Ice covers most of the island and glaciers abound. However the coastal zones remain ice-free during the summer and are home for an array of plant and animal life, including Elephant, Weddell and Leopard seals, and Chinstrap and Gentoo penguins.

HMS *Endurance* visits regularly and recent activities include a boat survey of Maxwell Bay at the south western end of the island. On this occasion hosting by the Korean research base enabled *Endurance* to depart on another task, leaving her boats to operate with support nearby. Such international cooperation is typical of the Antarctic, and as with other isolated places, *Endurance* and her crew regularly make contacts with the various nationalities on King George Island. Many extend invitations for crew members to visit their encampments: hospitality which is reciprocated by the *Endurance*.

Antarctica

Further south is the Antarctic continent itself. Beautiful, awe-inspiring yet menacing, much of the land is a high plateau, with extensive mountain ranges interspersed with valleys running to the sea. It holds some 90 per cent of the world's fresh water, albeit locked up in massive ice sheets that cover almost all of the land and large areas of sea. Icy winds and storms sweep continually over the continent, making both the ice and the seas around dangerous places to be.

Some coastal areas are not permanently ice-bound, but they only add up to about two per cent of the total land mass. Such land that is exposed is largely bare rock and scree, with only tiny amounts of vegetation able to survive. It may sound strange with so much ice around, but this continent is actually one of the driest places on earth.

Human habitation has been rare. Isolated whiling and sealing stations have been home for hardy mariners, but in the present day the only residents are scientists. This very isolation means that even though the natural environment is one of the toughest on earth, wildlife of all kinds thrives. Various species of penguin, seabird, seal and other animals populate the coastal zones, while shoals of fish and even whale pods all manage to exist in this place where the imprint of mankind is at its weakest.

Ice

Antarctica is covered by the largest single mass of ice on the planet. This ice sheet is usually identified as having two elements: the East Antarctic Ice Sheet of some 10 million square km (3.9 million square miles) which covers the Antarctic land mass; and the West Antarctic Ice Sheet of 2 million square km (0.8 million square miles) which rises from the sea bed.

These ice sheets change and renew themselves continuously. As new frost and snow crystals continually form on the surface, they compress the existing ice beneath them until the bottom layers form dense glacial ice. Under immense pressure this glacial ice acts more like a liquid and 'flows' downhill. In many valleys the ice forms glaciers, which eventually flow, into the sea. Some of these glaciers are huge – the biggest being the Lambert Glacier at 515 km (320 miles) long and over 50 km (31 miles) wide. It moves along at a rate of about 2.5 cm (1 inch) every day.

Shelves and bergs

An ice shelf is often formed where ice sheets and glaciers reach the sea. A shelf can be hundreds of metres thick and hundreds of kilometres across, with the free edge floating many kilometres out to sea. The largest is the Ross Ice Shelf, about the same size as France; while the Larsen shelf runs along the west side of the Antarctic peninsula and is nearly 400 km (250 miles) long.

CHAPTER FIVE - **Where She Goes**

CHAPTER FIVE - Where She Goes

The edges of the ice shelves are eroded by the sea and weather and eventually crack and wear down, although new ice continually pushes into them from the landward. Icebergs are formed (calved) when larger bits break off to float free. Such icebergs come in all sizes. The smallest, up to a few metres across, are known as 'growlers', while those a few metres larger are known as 'bergy bits'. Larger icebergs can be a serious threat to shipping, and mariners in these waters have to be continually alert for their presence. *Endurance* helps in this respect by detecting and monitoring those she comes across and reporting them to other ships in the area.

Sea Ice

But not all ice forms on land. In the winter months the surface of the sea itself freezes to form salty sea ice. This isn't as thick as the ice shelves, usually being only a few metres deep. The area covered by sea ice changes remarkably with the Antarctic seasons, growing from around 3 million square km (1.2 million square miles) in February to about 20 million square km (7.7 million square miles) in October – an area twice the size of Europe.

British Antarctic Territory

The British Antarctic Territory is one of the competing territorial claims to part of Antarctica. It is a triangular-shaped slice from the South Pole up to 60 degrees south, and bounded by longitudes 20 and 80 degrees west. It includes the Antarctic peninsula and the Weddell Sea and the landscape ranges from spectacular mountains, rugged coastline and islands to ice plains and ice shelves.

The territory is currently administered as an Overseas Dependent Territory, but the only occupants are the three British Antarctic Survey research stations. However, the territory does have its own legal system and issues its own postage stamps. Conflicting claims by Argentina and Chile overlap the region, although under the terms of the Antarctic Treaty, all territorial claims are suspended and all nations cooperate peacefully in the name of conservation and research.

The British Antarctic Survey

The British Antarctic Survey (BAS) maintains a portfolio of research programmes within the British Antarctic Territory and associated islands, with four all-year stations and numerous summer-only stations and field surveys.

THE RED PLUM   HMS Endurance

Chapter Five - Where She Goes

Britain has taken an interest in Antarctica and the surrounding oceans since the eighteenth century, although most exploration didn't take place until the early twentieth century. During the Second World War, the UK Government mounted Operation *Tabarin*, a military expedition to assert the UK's territorial claims and to deny the surrounding waters and harbours to enemy warships and submarines. *Tabarin* established bases, and as well as military operations, began collecting scientific observations. After the war the bases were transferred to a civilian organisation and expanded their scientific work. More bases opened (and closed) until the organisation became the BAS in 1962.

BAS has its headquarters in Cambridge, England, from which an extensive programme of research is managed. Over 400 staff take part in programmes at Rothera, Halley and Signy stations, at King Edward Point and Bird Island in South Georgia, and in various field surveys and expeditions. Most people only work in the field in the summer, although a small group of less than fifty overwinter at four of the stations.

The main objective of the BAS is to undertake a programme of scientific research and survey, whether alone or, increasingly, in close cooperation with other international research institutes. The BAS also has a role of maintaining British influence in Antarctic affairs, and raising public awareness of scientific and conservation issues.

The BAS has two ice-capable support ships. RRS *James Clark Ross* is an advanced research vessel, while RRS *Ernest Shackleton* provides support and resupply to BAS stations. The survey also has four ski-equipped Twin Otter aircraft that can land on ice-covered airstrips. A larger De Havilland Canada Dash 7 links Rothera base to the Falkland Islands and to the rest of the world. HMS *Endurance* works closely with the BAS, and her two helicopters are often used to deploy and support their field teams.

The Antarctic Charter

The Antarctic Treaty is one of the most successful international treaties ever agreed. In 1959, the 12 nations that had been active in Antarctic exploration signed an agreement where they committed to consult on the uses and exploitation of the continent and prevent it becoming a source of conflict or discord.

These original signatories (Argentina, Australia, Belgium, Chile, France, Japan, New Zealand, Norway, South Africa, United Kingdom, United States and USSR) have since been joined by many other nations who have agreed to follow the precepts of the original treaty.

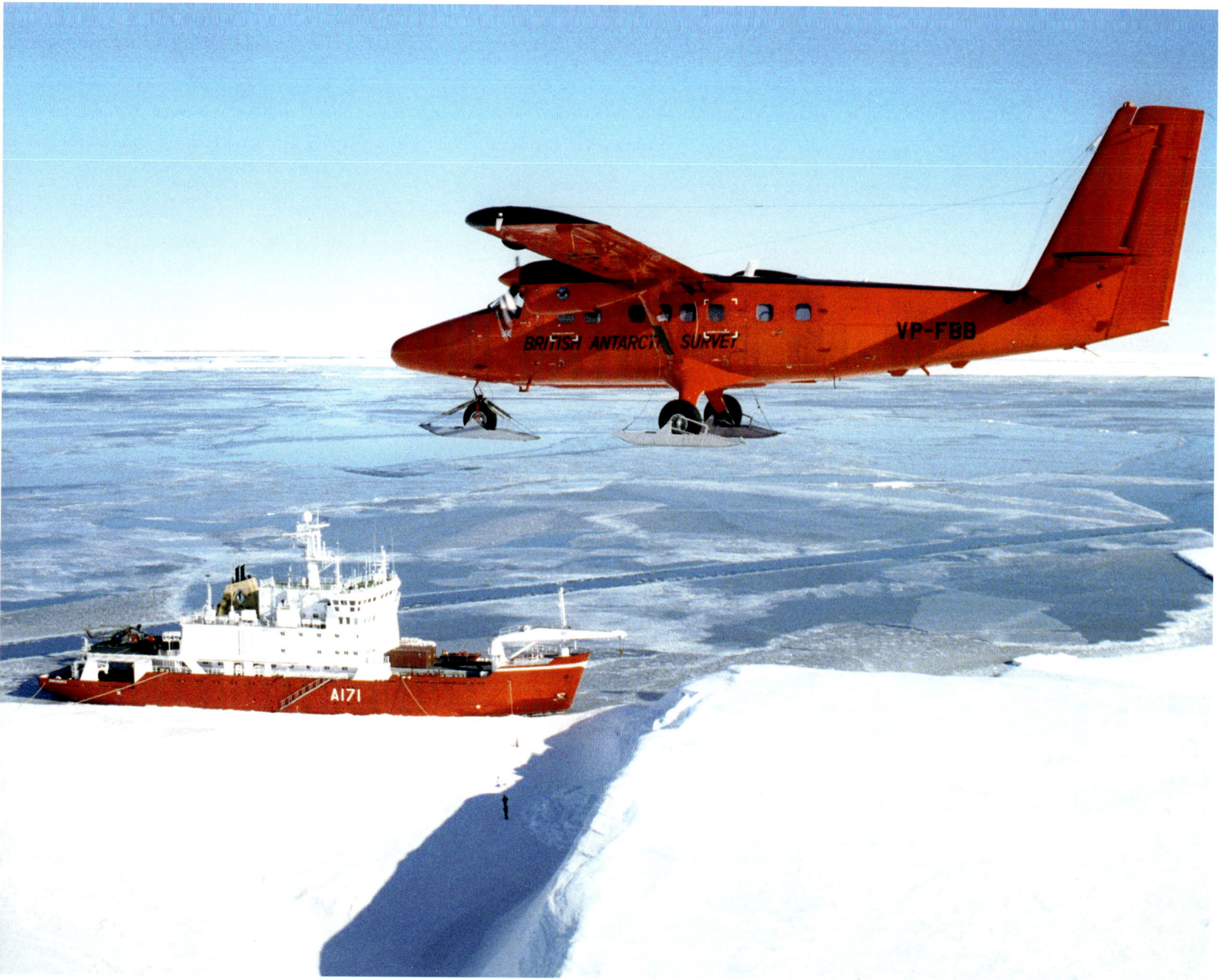
VP-FBB
A171

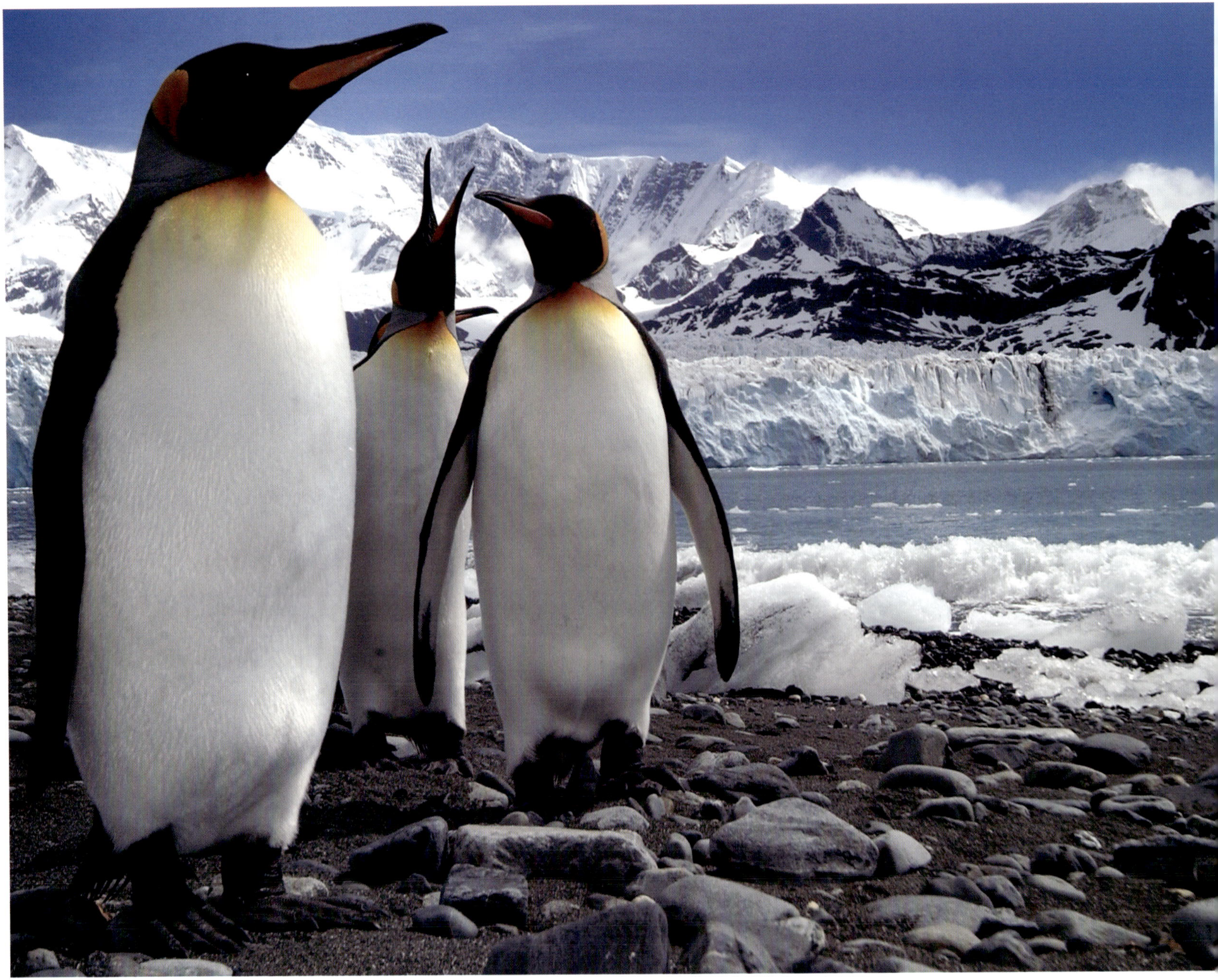

Chapter Five - Where She Goes

For such a wide-ranging international agreement, the treaty is remarkably short. It has 14 articles, where among other things, the signatories have agreed that:

- Antarctica will be used exclusively for peaceful purposes. No military activities are permitted.
- The freedom to conduct scientific research is guaranteed
- Signatories will cooperate in scientific research, will exchange plans and personnel and will make their results freely available.
- Disputes over sovereignty will set aside and no new claims made.
- Nuclear explosions or the disposal of radioactive waste are prohibited.
- Signatories will to allow observers to inspect their ships, stations and equipment to ensure the treaty is being observed.

The parties meet regularly to discuss Antarctic development and a number of additional agreements have since been created, mainly to enhance the protection of the Antarctic environment and ecology. This raft of agreements is known as the Antarctic Treaty System.

Other decision-making forums have been created, where specialised United Nations and international organisations play their part in the treaty system, providing advice and input on the conservation of plants and animals, preservation of the environment and historic sites, mapping and charting, and the issues created by the increase in tourism.

Tourism

Antarctic tourism is growing rapidly, with operators running cruises and expeditions to much of the coastline and many of the islands, mainly in the southern summer. As with most tourism it can be a two-edged sword. If handled well it enables people to see and marvel at this great wilderness and its teeming wildlife, and perhaps gain a new appreciation of the need to prevent its destruction. But if tourism is mishandled or uncontrolled it will bring about that very destruction.

Most of the operators who work in the region are affiliated to the International Association of Antarctic Tour Operators (IAATO), an industry body representing the interests of the growing tourist trade in Antarctica. IAATO also provides experts to the some of the Treaty forums and meetings. IAATO members follow guidelines adopted by the Antarctic Treaty partners to minimise the impact of their operations on the fabric of Antarctica. These guidelines are intended to protect wildlife, vegetation and the general environment, and to ensure that research programs

Chapter Five - Where She Goes

are not disrupted. Operators following the guidelines should provide advance notification of their activities, liaise with scientific stations and report on their expeditions afterwards. They are also expected to ensure that their passengers are properly supervised and that safety is carefully considered on each trip.

Endurance has recently hosted a team of inspectors from IAATO and five of the signatory governments, and taken them to visit some of the most important tourist and visitor sites within the treaty zone. Their remit was to check that tour operators were actually observing the agreed guidelines, and to examine the impact these operations on each site.

The Antarctic environment

The fact that Antarctica is relatively unpolluted and untouched by human activity means that it gives a superb window on the natural processes that have formed our world, our climate and how life has evolved.

Clean, weathered rocks uncovered by vegetation, animal traces or habitation show geologists the detailed structure of the terrain and provide evidence of the structure of the continent and how the earth was formed.

Biologists can study the undisturbed wildlife on land, in the air and at sea, and how it has adapted to severe weather conditions. The hardy vegetation can also be studied, and fragments trapped in the ice give clues to how plant life has evolved.

Antarctica can also tell us much about the earth's climate and how it has changed over the centuries. The very structure of the ice sheets and the pattern of ice crystals and air bubbles in the ice can be interpreted to give a picture of how temperatures and seasons have changed. Information has already been collected on changes over the last 400,000 years.

It is also clear that Antarctica itself plays a vital part in determining the world's climate. Ice insulates the sea from sunlight, keeping it and the Antarctic air cool. And when the sea ice melts in the summer it cools the ocean, an important factor in the weather pattern for the southern hemisphere. This melt water also encourages microscopic plants to grow on or near the ocean surface, providing the basic building block of the maritime food chain food which reaches up to the larger fish, birds and mammals at the higher end.

CHAPTER FIVE - **Where She Goes**

There is also evidence that changes in climate, especially the rise in global temperatures, are having their effect on the Antarctic environment itself. Part of the Larsen ice shelf collapsed in 1995, an event that attracted media publicity and acted as a warning signal and to many people around the world. And there is also evidence that the amount of sea ice that forms each year may be decreasing. If this happens the Southern Ocean will warm up, causing more ice to melt and the heating effect to increase.

Scientists can examine these effects. They can record, understand and publicise them. And *Endurance* plays a vital role here. But scientists alone cannot change what's happening. That's down to all of us. To preserve the pristine Antarctic environment and prevent the rise in global warming will take changes to our political, commercial industrial and personal behaviour. It's a tough challenge that we will have to meet as an international community.

Whether we achieve this or not remains to be seen. But we can't say we haven't been warned.

THE RED PLUM   93   **HMS Endurance**

Further information & Acknowledgements

You can find out more information about HMS *Endurance* and Antarctica from the following websites:

The Royal Navy's HMS Endurance site:
www.royalnavy.mod.uk/server/show/nav.1843

A fascinating site for schools where Endurance posts regular updates and information on her work and progress:
www.visitandlearn.co.uk

British Antarctic Survey
www.antarctica.ac.uk

The UK Hydrography Office
www.hydro.gov.uk

The Falklands Islands Government
www.falklands.gov.fk

South Georgia
www.sgisland.org

South Georgia Heritage Trust
www.sght.org

Deception Island
www.deceptionisland.aq

Heritage Antarctica
www.heritage-antarctica.org

The history of south-polar exploration
www.south-pole.com

International Association of Antarctic Tour Operators
www.iaato.org

Save the Albatross campaign
www.savethealbatross.net

To contact the publisher or purchase additional copies, visit:
www.coachhouseonline.co.uk

Acknowledgements

The publisher and author would like to thank all those on HMS *Endurance* and elsewhere who helped in the publication of this book. Special thanks go to:

Capt. Nick Lambert
Lt Cdr Carl Wiseman
Lt Cdr George Tabeart Surveyor
Lt Cdr Ian 'Buck' Taylor
Lt Matt Liddell
Lt Mark Jameson
Lt Emma Brown
Lt James Coleman
LA(Phot) Matt Ellison
Revd Steve Parselle
Peter Wordie for his kind permission, to use his fathers photographs on page 17 (all rights reserved)
And many thanks for the help and assistance of the Fleet Photographic Unit, Portsmouth

"Bon Voyage"